Success Sutras for Students

Stay Inspired!

Professor M.S.RAO, Ph.D.
International Leadership Guru

Foreword by
James M. Kouzes

ATLANTIC
PUBLISHERS & DISTRIBUTORS (P) LTD

Published by
ATLANTIC
PUBLISHERS & DISTRIBUTORS (P) LTD
7/22, Ansari Road, Darya Ganj,
New Delhi-110002
Phones : +91-11-40775252, 23273880, 23275880, 23280451
Fax : +91-11-23285873
web : www.atlanticbooks.com
e-mail : orders@atlanticbooks.com

Branch Office
5, Nallathambi Street, Wallajah Road,
Chennai-600002
Phones : +91-44-64611085, 32413319
e-mail : chennai@atlanticbooks.com

ISBN 978-81-269-1852-2

Printed in India at Nice Printing Press, A-33/3A, Site-IV,
Industrial Area, Sahibabad, Ghaziabad, U.P.

International Acclaim for Professor M.S.Rao's Book

"Tomorrow's leader begins as today's child, which is why I applaud Professor M.S.Rao's efforts in this new book to inspire the younger generation to succeed. He provides much practical wisdom and clear-headed strategic advice to help young people achieve their potential. By encouraging youths to dream big and liberate themselves from a pessimistic mindset, he offers a wealth of encouragement as well as specific tools to advance professionally and make a positive impact in the world. Professor M.S.Rao's passion for transforming negative thoughts into positive outcomes is on display throughout this uplifting, instructive text."

– Dipak C. Jain,
Dean, INSEAD

"Student success is a rare yet essential focus that the passionate international leadership educator, Professor M.S.Rao brings to new levels of understanding and appreciation in his book, *Success Sutras for Students: Stay Inspired!* I recommend reading this book."

– Frances Hesselbein

President & CEO, The Frances Hesselbein Leadership Institute (Formerly The Peter F. Drucker Foundation for Nonprofit Management); Former CEO, The Girl Scouts of the USA

"International leadership expert and speaker, Professor M.S.Rao, has come out with a new leadership book for students, *Success Sutras for Students: Stay Inspired!* This book contains interesting case studies, stories, anecdotes, and illustrations based on author's 32 years of experiences in various capacities. It calls upon students to be responsible citizens to make a difference in the lives of others."

– Dr. Tony Alessandra,
Hall-of-Fame Keynote Speaker and author of 28 books including The Platinum Rule®

"The international management thinker, Professor M.S.Rao has come out with yet another leadership book for students titled, *Success Sutras for Students: Stay Inspired!* It provides sage advices for students to dream big and lead from the front. It implores them to become responsible citizens. It is a must read!"

– James Strock,
Author, Serve to Lead, Theodore Roosevelt on Leadership, Reagan on Leadership.

"If you believe in youth, this book explains why. If you don't believe in youth, this book explains why you should believe in them. Great set of insights. This book shows the essence of mentoring, i.e. transferring wisdom by experience without losing the spirit of the young. As the book itself says: 'listen actively and ask questions. It gives so much hope for the next generation....'"

– Fons Trompenaars
Ranked # 42 Management Thinker in the world, Thinkers50

"The global management thinker, Professor M.S.Rao has come out with yet another leadership book *Success Sutras for Students: Stay Inspired!* It inspires students not only to dream but to do and achieve big. I strongly recommend reading this book, get your dreams down on paper and take action!"

– Bob Urichuck,

Internationally Recognized Sales Guru - Ranked # 4 in World's Top 30, following Zig Ziglar, Brian Tracy and Tom Hopkins

"Professor M.S.Rao inspires his students to dream and achieve in his powerful book *Success Sutras for Students: Stay Inspired!* He captures the essentials of success in dreaming big, building confidence, developing skills, and entrepreneurial thinking. In life, a person either hates losing enough to change or hates changing enough to lose. Professor Rao is a beacon of encouragement for his students to change and win!"

– Orrin Woodward: 2011 IAB Leader of the Year

"It's so important for students to be mindful of what practices contribute to enduring success. Professor M.S.Rao's book *Success Sutras for Students: Stay Inspired!* provides great examples and suggestions for cultivating a positive, forward-looking attitude."

Patricia Wheeler, Ph.D.,

Global Executive Coach, Managing Partner, The Levin Group LLC, Publisher, Leading News

"I love this book; I wish had a copy of it when I was a student. International management guru, Professor M.S.Rao's *Success Sutras for Students: Stay Inspired!* is a wonderful book filled with powerful teachings and wisdom. I read it with great enjoyment and know it will absolutely make you a more successful student and citizen."

– John Spence

One of the Top 100 Business Thought Leaders in America

"Professor M.S.Rao is offering excellent advice to students and future leaders in his new book, *Success Sutras for Students: Stay Inspired!* Packed with ideas and guidance on building a successful career, his new book will be a must-have resource for any student interested in pursuing an extraordinary life."

– Harrison Monarth,

Bestselling Author, Executive Presence and 360 Degrees of Influence

"Kudos to Professor M.S.Rao for giving students the gift of inspiration in his book, *Success Sutras for Students: Stay Inspired!* His commitment to a lifetime of service through the empowerment of others shines throughout this book, and the tips found within will provide practical wisdom for many!"

– Jane Hyun,

Global leadership strategist and coach, Author, Breaking the Bamboo Ceiling, Harpercollins

"Professor M.S.Rao's book truly inspires students to dream and achieve big. A must read for a future of achievement."

– Arthur F. Carmazzi,

World's Top Ten Leadership Guru and Founder of Directive Communication Psychology

Author of "Lessons from the Monkey King – Leading Change to Create Gorilla Sized Results"

"Professor M.S.Rao, the international leadership guru has come out with yet another leadership book *Success Sutras for Students: Stay Inspired!* This book equips students with tools and techniques to achieve quick career success and prepares them to face workplace challenges effectively. I strongly recommend reading this book."

– Terri Levine,

Best Selling Author, Coaching is for Everyone

"With his 20th book, *Success Sutras for Students: Stay Inspired!* Professor M.S.Rao has done it again! When your dreams are big your success can be just as big, and Professor Rao keeps showing students how."

– Barry Maher,

www.barrymaher.com, author, Filling the Glass

"Young students today often think they have all the answers and often ignore the opportunities to learn from more experienced and mature role models in their life. This book offers many great sutras for students to be successful and inspired."

– Lenny Laskowski,

International Professional speaker and author of the book, "Painless Presentations – The Proven Stress-Free Way to Successful Public Speaking" and "10 Days to More Confident Public Speaking"

Dedication

Dedicated to my father, Late M. Jagadeeswara Rao,
and his three brothers M. Venkataratnam,
M. Ramakrishna Rao and
M. Girivardana Rao

Foreword

A colleague of ours has a note taped to his computer that reads, "If you have not endured the most difficult, you cannot become the most successful." He keeps it there to remind him every day that achieving his hopes and aspirations is not going to be easy—nor should it be. In fact, it is just the opposite. Success is going to involve challenge, difficulty, adversity, and change. Success means running into brick walls and dead ends. It means finding yourself in dark places and down blind alleys. There is nothing easy about success.

But that's really the good news. No one ever got anything extraordinary done without overcoming major obstacles. No one ever built a profitable business, excelled at a competitive sport, cured a dreaded disease, liberated oppressed people, or created a sustainable community without being seriously tested. Hardships have a way of making people come face-to-face with what they really are and what they are capable of becoming. When times are stable and secure, nothing exceptional happens. They don't stretch you. They don't bring out your best. There is a clear connection between challenge and success.

The other good news is that you have this book, *Success Sutras for Students: Stay Inspired!* to help you. Another truth about success is that you can't do it alone. No one ever did. You need caring support and sound advice, and that is just what Professor M.S.Rao offers you. Here you will find proverbs, stories, and lessons about the essentials of success that inspire you, educate you, and carry you along the path. There is advice on how to cultivate the mind of an achiever, excel as a leader, build your own brand, be a responsible citizen, and a lot more. Name an ingredient in success, and you are likely to find it here.

And one other thing. Another person we interviewed for one of our books said to us: "Everything you need to be successful you already have." You ought to know. She started an environmental movement at the age of nine—that's right, she was nine years old when she took action. Under her leadership the organization grew to 350,000 members worldwide. Twenty years after she launched it she was named a Woman of Distinction for her pioneering efforts. Success is not something reserved for older people. It is independent of age. As our young friend says, "Everything you need you already have. It's all about taking the first step."

You don't have to look up for success. You don't have to look out for success. You only have to look within...and then take that first step.

I wish you all the very best on your adventures!

James M. Kouzes
Executive Fellow of Leadership
Leavey School of Business
Santa Clara University (USA)
Co-author of The Leadership Challenge, Credibility, A Leader's Legacy, and The Truth About Leadership

Preface

> "Finish each day and be done with it. You have done what you could; some blunders and absurdities have crept in; forget them as soon as you can. Tomorrow is a new day; you shall begin it serenely and with too high a spirit to be encumbered with your old nonsense."
>
> – Ralph Waldo Emerson

Welcome to *Success Sutras for Students: Stay Inspired!* You may be wondering why I am doing a book on students' success as I often author books on leadership. During my teaching and training programs I have come across students repeatedly asking me about the tools and techniques to succeed and to fast-track their careers. In addition, they have lots of concerns that remain unaddressed. In fact, they are looking for right guidance and direction to achieve all-round success in their lives. Hence, I have authored this book exclusively for students to address their concerns with clarifications.

The book begins with discovering your hidden potential followed by developing the mind of an achiever. It outlines that the achievers are ordinary individuals with extraordinary habits and practices. It explains leaders and leadership and implores to build leadership skills and abilities to excel as leaders. It describes SMART goals to hit the bull's eye. It coins career acumen and unveils the tools and techniques to fast-track your career. It offers sage advice to change your mindset and cross the thin line to achieve success.

The book contains debates between the people qualified from ordinary educational institutions and the people qualified from prestigious educational institutions. It is the X factor that decides the success of the individuals, not the institutional affiliations. It explains the significance of Pareto Principle and to effectively make use of time to achieve success by avoiding information overload and concentrating on what is really required. It encourages students to try entrepreneurship and become job providers rather than job seekers.

Currently soft skills are imperative to survive at each level of management. The book describes NLP (Neuro Linguistic Programming) that connects your unconscious and conscious mind to develop compatibility and chemistry with others to lead from the front successfully. It offers NLP questionnaire to help you assess what is true for you at various levels. It emphasizes on the importance of listening attentively to learn effectively and ensure successful communication. It underscores the importance of presenting positive body language to excel as leaders. It elaborates assertiveness and explains how to decline assertively for unreasonable requests at the workplace. It advises to be proficient and competent in the workplace to avoid massaging bosses' ego. It emphasizes to work with what you have rather than blaming the circumstances. It provides tools to make decisions wisely and techniques to build your leadership brand.

The book implores to love your mother but don't hate another person's mother, thus calling upon everyone to love all communities in the world. It enlightens you to be proud of being the citizen of your country. It concludes with becoming a responsible citizen by being duty-oriented rather than being right-oriented. The book outlines appendix containing the list of concerns with clarifications for students.

I hope this book will inspire you to make it a priority, learn as much as you can on career success to excel as a successful professional and, above all, a successful leader.

M.S.Rao

Acknowledgments

Writing a book is never a solo project. I am deeply indebted to many people whose expertise, wisdom, and encouragement kept me going. My wife's and children's (Ganesh Sai and Ramakrishna Sayee) encouragement and sacrifice made this book possible, and for that I am forever thankful. My wife, Padmavathy is a symbol of sacrifice and support for my books, and also is an immeasurable blessing in my life.

Several quotes, examples and anecdotes are the result of a collection from different sources. It is practically impossible to acknowledge each one of them separately. While I have tried to give credit wherever it is due, in case I have missed anything, I will give due credit in future editions if it is brought to my notice.

I thank everyone including the team of Atlantic Publishers and Distributors Pvt. Ltd. for publication of this book. I specifically thank Harjeet Singh, Publication Coordinator for his coordination in publication of this book.

I express special thanks to all the readers who graciously took time off from their busy schedules to write to me, and share their views, and offer feedback on my books.

M.S.Rao

Quotes

"Humanity has only scratched the surface of its real potential." – Peace Pilgrim

"Concentration of effort and the habit of working with a definite chief aim are two of the essential factors in success which are always found together. One leads to the other." – Napoleon Hill

"The error of youth is to believe that intelligence is a substitute for experience, while the error of age is to believe experience is a substitute for intelligence." – Ernest Hemingway

"By education I mean that training in excellence from youth upward which makes a man passionately desire to be a perfect citizen, and teaches him to rule, and to obey, with justice. This is the only education which deserves the name." – Plato

"I don't think you ever will yourself to win. I think you prepare yourself the best you can, get yourself in the best mindset you can get in, and go after it." – Jack Nicklaus

"Training is such a vital part of preparation for a game, you really do train to play. It tops up your ability, like sharpening a carving knife. You can get away with not doing it for a while, as long as you have reached a certain standard of fitness." – Graeme Le Saux

"People who thrive put in at least 1000 hours of sustained, consistent training to reach their potential." – Malcolm Gladwell

"You can teach a student a lesson for a day; but if you can teach him to learn by creating curiosity, he will continue the learning process as long as he lives." – Clay P. Bedford

"Your own mind is a sacred enclosure into which nothing harmful can enter except by your promotion." – Ralph Waldo Emerson

"The mind is its own place, and in itself can make a heaven of Hell, a hell of Heaven." – John Milton

"The mind is a wonderful servant, but a terrible master." – Robin Sharma

"Effective questioning brings insight, which fuels curiosity, which cultivates wisdom." – Chip Bell

"Curiosity is the catalyst for motivation." – Tony Richards

"A person without a goal is like a ship without a rudder." – Denis Waitley

"We are the creative force of our life, and through our own decisions rather than our conditions, if we carefully learn to do certain things, we can accomplish those goals." – Stephen Covey

"The human body is the best picture of the human soul." – Ludwig Wittgenstein

"No man should judge unless he asks himself in absolute honesty whether in a similar situation he might not have done the same." – Viktor Frankl

"We must do all that we can, to give our children the best in education and social upbringing – for while they are the youth of today, they shall be the leaders of tomorrow." – John F. Kennedy

"The critical ingredient is getting off your butt and doing something. It's as simple as that. A lot of people have ideas, but there are few who decide to do something about them now. Not tomorrow. Not next week. But today. The true entrepreneur is a doer, not a dreamer." – Nolan Bushnell

"The winners in life think constantly in terms of I can, I will, and I am. Losers, on the other hand, concentrate their waking thoughts on what they should have or would have done, or what they can't do." – Dennis Waitley

"Leadership is practiced not so much in words as in attitude and in actions." – Harold Geneen

"We do not grow by knowing all of the answers, but rather by living with the questions." — Max De Pree

"The only limitation in your life is the limitation of your own thinking." – James A. Ray

"We are limited but we can push back the borders of our limitations" – Stephen R. Covey

"We can teach a lot of things, but if the teacher can't relate by talking to a group of friendly students, he'll never be a competent teacher." – William Glasser

"Whenever you're in conflict with someone, there is one factor that can make the difference between damaging your relationship and deepening it. That factor is attitude." – William James

"A teacher's purpose is not to create students in his own image, but to develop students who can create their own image." – Author Unknown

"Only undertake what you can do in an excellent fashion. There are no prizes for average performance." – Brian Tracy

"The secret of achievement is to hold a picture of a successful outcome in the mind." – Henry David Thoreau

"Success is how high you bounce when you hit bottom." – General George Patton

"Success consists of going from failure to failure without loss of enthusiasm." – Winston Churchill

"Our ego hinders our ability to influence more than anything else under our control." – Michael McKinney

"When all is said and done, teaching is what I try to do for a living." – Jack Welch

"Effective leadership is not about making speeches or being liked; leadership is defined by results, not attributes." – Peter Drucker

"Writing is a way of talking without being interrupted." – Jules Renard

"Thrive on risk as a part of life." – Denis Waitley

"Be willing to launch in faith, with no guarantees of success. This is the mark of personal greatness." – Brian Tracy

"Be like the turtle. If he didn't stick his neck out, he wouldn't get anywhere at all." – Harvey Mackay

"If the creator had a purpose in equipping us with a neck, he surely meant us to stick it out." – Arthur Koestler

"Well, when you're trying to create things that are new, you have to be prepared to be on the edge of risk." – Michael Eisner

"The bad news is time flies. The good news is you're the pilot." – Michael Altshuler

"In dwelling, live close to the ground. In thinking, keep to the simple. In conflict, be fair and generous. In governing, don't try to control. In work, do what you enjoy. In family life, be completely present." – Lao Tzu

"Reflect on your present blessings, of which every man has many; not on your past misfortunes, of which all men have some." – Charles Dickens

"I don't think of the past. The only thing that matters is the everlasting present." – W. Somerset Maugham

"What the caterpillar calls the end, the rest of the world calls a butterfly." – Lao Tzu

"I am personally convinced that one person can be a change catalyst, a 'transformer' in any situation, any organization. Such an individual is yeast that can leave an entire loaf. It requires vision, initiative, patience, respect, persistence, courage, and faith to be a transforming leader." – Stephen R. Covey

"One key to successful leadership is continuous personal change. Personal change is a reflection of our inner growth and empowerment." – Robert E. Quinn

"Luck is what happens when preparation meets opportunity." – Seneka

"Great leaders are not born, they are developed...fired in the crucible of experience and opportunity." – Aristotle

"Out of clutter, find simplicity. From discord, find harmony. In the middle of difficulty lies opportunity." – Albert Einstein

"If the career you have chosen has some unexpected inconvenience, console yourself by reflecting that no career is without them." – Jane Fonda

"One of life's most painful moments comes when we must admit that we didn't do our homework, that we are not prepared." – Merlin Olsen

"It is better to be prepared for an opportunity and not have one than to have an opportunity and not be prepared." – Whitney Young, Jr.

"Good teaching is one-fourth preparation and three-fourths theatre." – Gail Goldwin

"I honestly think it is better to be a failure at something you love than to be a success at something you hate." – George Burns

"Defeat is not the worst of failures. Not to have tried is the true failure." – George Woodberry

"When I was young, I observed that nine out of 10 things I did were failures, so I did 10 times more work." – George Bernard Shaw

"Failure is only postponed success as long as courage coaches ambition. The habit of persistence is the habit of victory." – Herbert Kaufman

"The great dividing line between success and failure can be expressed in five words: "I did not have time."– Franklin Field

"Entrepreneurs average 3.8 failures before final success. What sets the successful ones apart is their amazing persistence" – Lisa M. Amos

"There are no mistakes or failures, only lessons." – Denis Waitley

"It's fine to celebrate success but it is more important to heed the lessons of failure." – Bill Gates

"We are the creative force of our life, and through our own decisions rather than our conditions, if we carefully learn to do certain things, we can accomplish those goals." – Stephen Covey

"The reason most major goals are not achieved is that we spend our time doing second things first." – Robert J. McKain

"When successful people write down goals, announce these goals to respected colleagues and involve the colleagues in helping them improve (in a supportive way), positive measurable change is much more likely to occur." – Marshall Goldsmith

"We don't accomplish anything in this world alone...and whatever happens is the result of the whole tapestry of one's life and all the weavings of individual threads from one to another that creates something." – Sandra Day O'Connor

"To lead is to make an emotional connection on a very real and human level in every interaction." – Gary Burnison

"To be what we are, and to become what we are capable of becoming, is the only end in life." – Robert L. Stevenson

"Learning is an active process. We learn by doing. Only knowledge that is used sticks in your mind." – Dale Carnegie

"Learning is finding out what you already know, Doing is demonstrating that you know it, Teaching is reminding others that they know it as well as you do. We are all learners, doers, and teachers." – Richard David Bach

"Over the long run, superior performance depends on superior learning." – Peter Senge.

"Learning without thought is labor lost; thought without learning is perilous." – Confucius

"We are judged by what we finish, not what we start." – Anonymous

"Don't judge each day by the harvest you reap, but by the seeds you plant." – Robert Louis Stevenson

"Some of us will do our jobs well and some will not, but we will all be judged by only one thing – the result." – Vince Lombardi

"Respect for ourselves guides our morals; respect for others guides our manners." – Laurence

"What is tolerance? It is the consequence of humanity. We are all formed of frailty and error; let us pardon reciprocally each other's folly – that is the first law of nature."– Voltaire

"Personal development is your springboard to personal excellence. Ongoing, continuous, non–stop personal development literally assures you that there is no limit to what you can accomplish." – Brian Tracy

"Strength lies in differences, not in similarities." – Stephen Covey

"Your success in life isn't based on your ability to simply change. It is based on your ability to change faster than your competition, customers and business." – Mark Sanborn

"Success isn't about being a hero. It's about going to work every day, loving your job, loving your company, loving your fellow employees, and loving your customers." – Jim Parker, CEO of South West Airlines

"The roots of education are bitter, but the fruit is sweet." – Aristotle

"If you think education is expensive, try ignorance." – Derek Bok

"The secret of achievement is to hold a picture of a successful outcome in the mind." – Henry David Thoreau

"Be a yardstick of quality. Some people aren't used to an environment where excellence is expected." – Steve Jobs

"Look for an occupation that you like, and you will not need to labor for a single day in your life." – Confucius

"He who loves the world as his own body may be entrusted with the empire." – Lao Tzu

"When you sell a man a book you don't sell him just 12 ounces of paper and ink and glue – you sell him a whole new life." – Christopher Morley

"In life, don't be in a hurry, just walk slowly but surely and you will certainly encounter an unexpected, perplexing, dumbfounding moments in your journey." – Jehan Fostanes Nayga

"Learn to embrace change in your work and personal life and make the transition to a better you." – Author Unknown

"It is not work that kills men; it is worry. Worry is rust upon the blade." – Henry Ward Beecher

"It's a paradox. How does one balance living in the now with preparing responsibly for the future? The key to this dilemma lies in the distinction between 'worrying about the future', and 'preparing for the future'. The two concepts are not at all the same." – Jonathan Lockwood Huie

"A time for everything: A time to relax and a time to be busy, a time to frolic and a time to labor, a time to receive and a time to give, a time to begin and a time to finish." – Jonathan Lockwood Huie

"To live is to choose. But to choose well, you must know who you are and what you stand for, where you want to go and why you want to get there." – Kofi Annan

"An investment in knowledge pays the best interest." – Benjamin Franklin

Contents

1

Identify the Spark Within You

> *"You can be anything you want to be, if only you believe with sufficient conviction and act in accordance with your faith; for whatever the mind can conceive and believe, the mind can achieve."*
>
> –Napoleon Hill

Welcome to *Success Sutras for Students: Stay Inspired!* I have authored this book to provide suggestions for students. During my academic experience I found that the students are beset with several concerns and need clarifications. Some of the concerns don't have any substance and while some have valid substance. Hence, have I authored this book purely from the perspective of students to address their concerns; provide career guidance; and prepare them to face the corporate world.

The book helps students develop their personality and enhance their employment opportunities. In fact, currently the students are much sharper and smarter with the impact of technology and to prepare them is a major challenge for educators. Students face stiff competition in the workplace also as most of them are smart with great expectations.

Swami Vivekananda—A Symbol of Youth Power

> "The greatest sin is to think yourself weak. The remedy of weakness is not brooding over weakness, but thinking of strength."
>
> –*Swami Vivekananda*

When we talk 'power of youth' we recall Swami Vivekananda who is associated with Indian youth, and India celebrates 'national youth day' as a mark of respect towards this legend. Nowadays, some youth are misled due to degeneration values and ethics. They are often intoxicated by impatience and intolerance. They must draw inspiration from Swami Vivekananda whose speech on September 11, 1893 at Parliament of Religions in Chicago is memorable in the history of India. The speech has made a profound impact on the West. The speech symbolizes India's tolerance toward other religions and communities, and India's acceptance to assimilate all religions in its fold with magnanimity.

Swami Vivekananda was the first Indian in modern India who highlighted Hinduism in a true perspective to the West, and the latter accepted his views wholeheartedly. The American newspapers praised Swami Vivekanada's speech. *The New York Herald* wrote, "Vivekananda is undoubtedly the greatest figure in the Parliament of Religions. After hearing him we feel how foolish it is to send missionaries to this learned nation."

Swami Vivekananda represented India's face globally. He preached for universal brotherhood. Commenting on his perspectives and presentation, French Nobel Laureate, Romain Rolland said, "Swami Vivekananda's words are great music, phrases in the style of Beethoven, stirring rhythms like the march of Handel choruses."

You Have the Power Within You!

At times, some youth are beset with pessimism and cynicism. They must realize that they have a huge potential lying hidden within them. They must know how to realize and channel it effectively. When others can do it why cannot they? They must come out of their mental limitations and barriers. They must be positive, and must have an open mind.

The difference between the successful people and the unsuccessful people is that the success people know the tools and techniques and adopt as per the situation whereas the unsuccessful don't know them. And successful people focus on their strengths and unsuccessful people brood about their weaknesses. Hence, there is a need to acquire the tools and techniques to succeed in life. In fact, we humans don't know how to tap our inner potential. We are beset with several mental limitations. When we overcome such mental limitations and barriers we can achieve everything in this world. Remember that we have so much energy locked inside of us. Our human mind is incredibly powerful. We must know how to realize, channel and exploit it fully. Here are the tools and techniques to unlock your hidden potential:

- Surround with positive people.
- Convert your negative thoughts into positive thoughts by focusing on positive aspects.
- Look at the ideas, not the individuals.
- Convert your inner dialogue from negative to positive.
- Keep motivational quotes around you.
- Seek professional advice when encountered with repeated negative thoughts.
- Develop the attitude of gratitude.
- Don't look for a hero in others. Instead, look for a hero within yourself.

Remember that success is not permanent and failure is not final. Life is full of peaks and valleys. Don't get dejected with failures, and don't get excited with success. Always stay level headed with humility.

Believe in Yourself

Have faith in yourself. Believe in your talents. Norman Vincent Peale rightly remarked, "Believe in yourself! Have faith in your abilities! Without a humble but reasonable confidence in your own powers you cannot be successful or happy." Program your mind. Unlock your infinite hidden power. Your success depends on your thoughts and you can control your thoughts the way you want. Samuel Smiles said,

> "Sow a thought, and you reap an act;
>
> Sow an act, and you reap a habit;

Sow a habit, and you reap a character;
Sow a character, and you reap a destiny."

Take Feedback

You need to take feedback regularly to grow. Your feedback should not lower your self-esteem. Remember that your self-criticism is your feedback. Nobody can put you down unless you put down yourself. Eleanor Roosevelt rightly said, "No one can make you feel inferior without your consent." Don't get dejected by criticism. Take it in your stride and move on with confidence and mettle. Everything is there in your mind. If you think you are successful, you are successful. You can achieve anything and everything in this world. Dream big and achieve big!

Develop a great attitude because your attitude determines your altitude of success. To acquire a great attitude, replace the negative thoughts in your mind with positive thoughts. Set goals so that you can stay focused clearly. You can manage your time. You can enhance longevity. Above all, you can provide meaning to your life through goal-setting.

Convert Your Scars into Stars

Convert your weaknesses into strengths. Don't look at the door that is closed. Look at the door that is open. Remember what Swami Vivekananda said, "All great undertakings are achieved through mighty obstacles. Keep up the deepest mental poise. Take not even the slightest notice of what puerile creatures may be saying against you. Arise, awake and stop not till the goal is reached."

Stay Inspired!

Stay inspired from the messages of Swami Vivekananda. You are rightly placed in the history of India! Mother India is calling you to shoulder the leadership roles and responsibilities. Make your mother India proud by unlocking your hidden potential. You have the power within you. Unlock your potential. Explore, experiment, and grow. Prove yourself the best. Make your parents proud, and make your country proud. You were born to stand out. Remember the sage words of spiritual teachers, Ed and Deb Shapiro: "In every moment, no matter what is going on, you have the power within you to transform both yourself and your life."

We will discuss in detail about the success sutras and sage advices for students to succeed personally, professionally and socially in the following chapters.

> "Always give your best, never get discouraged, never be petty; always remember, others may hate you, but those who hate you don't win unless you hate them, and then you destroy yourself."
>
> –*Richard Nixon*

Remember: *Stay inspired!*

REFERENCES

Author's Facebook Page: http://www.facebook.com/pages/Professor-MSRao/451516514937414?skip_nax_wizard=true.

Author's Speaker Mix: http://speakermix.com/professor-m-s-rao.

Author's Blogs:

http://professormsraoguru.blogspot.com

http://professormsrao.blogspot.com

http://profmsr.blogspot.com

2

Cultivate the Mind of an Achiever

"Only one who devotes himself to a cause with his whole strength and soul can be a true master. For this reason mastery demands all of a person"

–Albert Einstein

Do achievers have a unique mind? Are achievers extraordinary individuals? Is it tough to excel as an achiever? If your answer is "no" to all these questions, you are correct. In fact, achievers are like any other ordinary individuals but they have a specific set of traits, acquire skills and achieve greatness. They work hard, smart and wise to achieve their goals and hence, they stand out. Above all, it is not tough to excel as an achiever, if you pursue your passion; follow the road less traveled; and are willing to wait for results. Therefore, in this chapter, we will discuss the characteristics of achievers and their mindset and what it takes to become an achiever.

Always think about the possibilities in your life. Have an open mind and look for opportunities around you. Often the opportunities come in the form of threats and if you can identify and exploit them, you can excel as an achiever. Never blame the circumstances. Be an optimist and work with what you have, and be resourceful.

Visualize yourself as an achiever. Visualization is a powerful tool to motivate yourself. It is rightly said that a battle is won twice, first in mind and then in reality. Think in your mind that you are successful. Think that everything is possible in the world. When you think in that way, your mind persuades your body and your actions will start in the direction to achieve success.

"The journey of thousand miles starts with a first single step," goes the proverb. When you take the first step you gain momentum for further journey and you can successfully reach your goals. Here are some of the qualities of achievers:

- Attitude determines your altitude. Attitude is a thin line that separates successful ones and unsuccessful ones. Hence, acquire positive, right and strong attitude to win.
- Follow the road less travelled. Robert Frost once said, "Two roads diverged in a wood and I–I took the one less traveled by." If you enter into the crowded areas, you get into rat race and remain like any other ordinary individual. Hence, choose the areas that have the least competition and move in that direction to stand out.
- Spot your talents. Everyone is blessed with talents through heredity. Through self-analysis and psychological tests, find out the same and pursue them.
- Acquire skills related to your talents. People often build skills and they align their talents which is a retrograde step. Hence, build skills and abilities around your talents to achieve quick success.
- Focus on your goals. When you look at great leaders and entrepreneurs they focused on what they wanted. Whether you look at Steve Jobs, Thomas Edison, and Alexander Graham Bell, they all clearly focused on their goals and hit the bull's eye. Hence, focus is the key to your success.
- Manage distractions. You find a lot of obstructions and distractions on your way to success. Prepare mentally about them and eliminate them as and when they stop you to keep yourself on the right track and on the fast track.

- Have self-discipline. All great achievers are self-disciplined and that made them stand out.
- Be committed to your tasks. Commitment is the key to your success. Once you decided to achieve your goals you must stay committed firmly.
- Set your priorities. You must learn how to manage your time by setting the priorities properly. You must differentiate between the chalk and the cheese.
- Forget your unpleasant past. Often your unpleasant past will hold you back from achieving your success. It consumes your 30 percent of your precious time. If you can learn lessons and forget your unpleasant past you can enhance your success rate as you find more time to concentrate on your current activities.
- Emphasize on excellence. Remember that excellence is an attitude you must cultivate. Don't worry about perfection as nobody is perfect in this world. Keep improving yourself constantly in your area of interest to excel as an expert.
- Stick to ethics and etiquette. Observe etiquette and follow ethics as both are two sides of the same coin and one without the other has no meaning.
- Maintain confidentiality. There are certain things to be kept confidential to excel as an achiever. And you must know what to veil and unveil. Super-achievers keep precious things close to their chest to avoid cut-throat competition.
- Learn constantly. Remember the Chinese proverb, "Learning is a treasure that will follow its owner everywhere." All super-achievers are constantly learners and they update constantly.
- Take feedback. Ken Blanchard said, "Feedback is the breakfast of champions". Hence, take feedback positively to identify your blind spots and improve for betterment.

- Work hard, smart and wise. These days, people are more intelligent and competitive as lots of information is thrown open on the internet. Therefore, you must learn what to choose carefully and follow the smart strategies wisely to become an achiever.
- Learn to lose a battle to win a war. The achievers are risk takers and are high in animal spirits. They don't mind losing for petty things to achieve pretty things in their lives.
- Be persistent. Don't give up when confronted with failures. Learn lessons and move on with renewed energy and enthusiasm.
- Build network with likeminded people. Connections help put you in the right place at the right time with the right people. Hence, become a member in clubs and associations in your area of interest to connect with the right people to grow professionally.
- Manage your time by balancing your personal, professional and social life. It is very challenging but it is possible if you want to enjoy a meaningful and successful life.
- Enjoy the journey to reach your goals. Although you emphasize on your destination enjoy the every moment of your journey to avoid regrets at the end of your life for not having enjoyed your life fully. Above all, you have one life to lead. Hence, lead your life happily and qualitatively.
- Make a difference in the lives of others. Help the people around you as best as you can. Bring out qualitative difference among them and they remember you beyond your lifetime.

Follow the outlined tips and cultivate the mind of an achiever and become an achiever. When others can achieve success, why cannot you achieve it? Be optimistic; prepare thoroughly and soar like an eagle. To conclude, in the words of Jean-Paul Sarte, "Man is fully responsible for his nature and choices."

"Limitations live only in our minds. But if we use our imaginations, our possibilities become limitless."

–Jamie Paolinetti, American Schroeder Iron Pro Cycling

Remember: *Be an achiever.*

3

Excel as a Leader

"Men make history and not the other way around. In periods where there is no leadership, society stands still. Progress occurs when courageous, skillful leaders seize the opportunity to change things for the better."

–Harry Truman

Students must build leadership skills and abilities to grow successfully. They must learn what leadership is, and must spot the opportunities to build leadership skills within the educational institutions. It helps them lead successfully in the corporate world thus achieving professional success. We will discuss the same in this chapter.

Before learning leadership students must debunk several myths about 'leadership' and 'leaders'. Here are the few myths —only experienced can excel as leaders; leaders are born; great communicators can alone become leaders; women cannot excel as leaders, etc. The truth is that age is not a constraint to excel as a leader; leaders are made; leadership is a holistic one, not confined to communication skills alone; and gender is not a deterrent to excel as leaders. After busting myths students must read various books, observe other successful leaders, experiment, explore and practice regularly to grow as leaders.

What is Leadership?

There are several definitions about 'leadership' and 'leader', and if you Google you get half a billion hits on these two terms. Some leadership gurus defined leadership as example, influence, not authority, and walking the talk, etc. For instance, John C. Maxwell said, "All leadership is influence." Ordway Tead said, "Leadership is the activity of influencing people to cooperate toward some goal which they come to find desirable." Dwight Eisenhower defined, "Leadership is the art of getting someone else to do something you want done because he wants to do it." Michael McKinney said, "Leadership is intentional influence." And Peter Drucker defined, "Leadership is not magnetic personality, that can just as well be a glib tongue. It is not "making friends and influencing people", that is flattery. Leadership is lifting a person's vision to higher sights, the raising of a person's performance to a higher standard, the building of a personality beyond its normal limitations." We can, therefore, define leadership as the process of setting vision, influencing people, forming teams, making decisions, motivating people constantly by allaying their apprehensions and aligning their energies and efforts to achieve organizational goals and objectives.

Emphasize on Extracurricular Activities

Developing leadership skills helps students acquire people skills and soft skills; develop team spirit; make decisions properly; manage complexity and uncertainty; and balance both bouquets and brickbats. Hence, educational institutions must emphasize on curricular and extracurricular activities equally to prepare students as well-rounded personalities. Emphasizing on extracurricular activities such as sports and games among students promote emotional intelligence, flexibility, adaptability, physical fitness, mental agility, leadership qualities, and above all, fraternity. Emphasizing on curricular activities equips them with hard skills and on extracurricular activities with soft skills. In fact, a judicious blend of soft and hard skills is essential to excel as successful personalities. However, most of the Indian educational institutions emphasize more on curricular rather than extracurricular activities resulting in lopsided personalities. Hence, educational institutions must emphasize on extracurricular activities to build leaders who can face corporate and life challenges with confidence.

Role of Educators in Grooming Students as Leaders

Benjamin Disraeli once said, "The greatest good you can do for another is not just share your riches, but to reveal to him his own." Therefore, educators must play a crucial role to groom students as leaders. Students need inspiring examples with interesting anecdotes to learn leadership in the classroom. It serves as a good theoretical base for students. Students must take active part in various group activities in their educational institutions such as organizing conference papers, meetings, picnics, and participating in role-plays under the supervision of passionate educators to build leadership skills and abilities. The educators must guide and groom them through mentoring and constant supervision. They must encourage students to explore and experiment various things. The educators must inspire students constantly by setting example and through inspiring stories of successful leaders. They must also conduct team building activities within the educational institutions or river rafting, trekking or mountaineering outside the educational institutions which help them develop emotional intelligence quotient (EQ) and cultivate the habit of give and take and flexibility. They must encourage students to come out of their comfort zones and apply various pressures with a view to toughen them to face challenges in their lives head-on.

How to Excel as a Leader?

Leadership is a complex discipline. It requires lots of learning and, above all, tons of practice. That is the reason leadership is widely talked about but least understood. John C. Maxwell once said, "Leadership develops daily, not in a day." In addition, it is proven that leadership can be taught. The reason is that leadership is based mostly on EQ and you can cultivate EQ through various sources but mostly through practice. When you want to excel as a leader, you must read good books. Take successful leaders as your role models. Find out what made them succeed as leaders. Apply them into practice. Read good books where you get inputs that help you learn leadership theoretically. Practice in your life and you get to know the practical problems and learn several things from your experience. You can also learn from the experiences of others through books. When you practice you make mistakes; fail and fall and then bounce back with tenacity and resilience. Keep trying in this way. Don't force people, but influence them. Don't talk much with people, but set an example. Don't blame them when things go wrong, but accept the blame so that people around you trust and follow. Don't demand respect, but command respect from others. Keep others' interests above your interests. When you do in this way you will excel as a successful leader. Above all, remember that leadership is not bestowed, but earned.

> "The growth and development of people is the highest calling of leadership."
>
> —*Harvey S. Firestone*

Remember: *Practice leadership.*

4

Acquire Career Acumen

"I have always advised my children and students not to worry so much about saving money or about climbing up the next run on the ladder of their career, an attitude which seems to be an obsession with highly motivated people, concerned about economic security. It is much more important to work at perfecting yourself and thereby ensure your usefulness no matter what fate does to you."

– Hans Seyle, in *The Stress of Life*

The caption 'career acumen' seems to be strange right! It is like business acumen and technical acumen where people have aptitude for business and technical aspects respectively. Nowadays, career aspirants must acquire career acumen to achieve career success and advancement. If you have clear idea about your career and the opportunities available at your hand, you will have wider employment opportunities and you can stand out from others. In addition, you will enjoy financial freedom, luxuries and have a competitive edge over your competitors and lead your life successfully.

What is Career Acumen?

Career acumen is about having a broad idea about your passion towards specific careers and their future. It includes your awareness about the careers with the pros and cons and longevity. The entire process is easier said than done. In order to find out your career acumen, you have to do research about yourself such as what kind of personality you are; and the type of careers that suit you. After finding them out, you must shortlist the careers that are close to your heart, and the ones that have the least competition. It is like starting your own business. When you want to start a business you have to do extensive research to find out the different businesses and their viability and longevity. At the same time, you must maintain the secrecy about your business to stay in the race for a longer time. These days, secrets cannot be maintained for a long time as the technology has made the world small and open. Hence, you must keep things confidential about your business and innovate constantly to stay ahead of your competitors. Similarly, you must do tons of research to find out the careers looking for longevity and exploring various options based on your passion as you spend most of your time on your career. Laurence G. Boldt rightly said, "The decisions you make about your work life are especially important, since most people spend more of their waking lives working than doing anything else. Your choices will affect, not only yourself and those closest to you, but in some way the whole world." As the battle is won twice—first in your mind and then in your real life, you must have a mental blueprint about the careers that you choose and work on them constantly to stand out from others.

Traditionally, there are 4 As—Attitude, Aptitude, Abilities and Awareness to roll out your career blueprint to grab employment opportunities. The career acumen covers all these 4 As with a scientific approach to ensure successful career outcomes. There are sunrise and sunset sectors. Hence, explore sunrise sectors and research on the areas that would have tremendous potential from 20 – 30 years of time. Identify and investigate those areas by gradually narrowing down the key sectors that provide you promising careers with financial benefits. Whether you want to be a job seeker or job provider, it helps you greatly if you adopt this strategy.

In my own case, I did my MBA very long ago when this degree was not in great demand. It helped me after 15 years as the demand for MBA grew greatly. Similarly, I started doing PhD in soft skills 5 years ago when this discipline was evolving, and I acquired my doctoral qualification in 2011. Now I am getting a lot of employment opportunities as there are a few people who have doctoral qualification in soft skills. However, I enjoy providing soft skills programs independently with my own company – MSR Leadership Consultants India. Similarly, you must do tons of research before pursuing your career. First of all, find out your passion and shortlist the careers with huge opportunities so that you will face the least competition. At the same time, don't get complacent as presently people are highly knowledgeable and competitive, and they can easily enter into your area thus crowding your career. Hence, do extensive research and shift from orbit to another and become a trailblazer. To conclude, the career aspirants must do research, acquire career acumen and follow the road less travelled to have a successful career and reach top positions smartly and quickly.

> "Analyzing what you haven't got as well as what you have is a necessary ingredient of a career."
>
> *–Orison Swett Marden*

Remember: *Follow the road less travelled.*

5

Enhance Your Employability

"You can give lifetime employability by training people, by making them adaptable, making them mobile to go other places to do other things. But you can't guarantee lifetime employment."

– Jack Welch

"Across the nine countries that are the focus of this report (Brazil, Germany, India, Mexico, Morocco, Turkey, Saudi Arabia, the United Kingdom, and the United States), only 43 percent of employers surveyed agreed that they could find enough skilled entry-level workers. This problem is not likely to be a temporary blip; in fact, it will probably get much worse. The McKinsey Global Institute estimates that by 2020 there will be a global shortfall of 85 million high and middle-skilled workers." The McKinsey Global Institute (www.mckinsey.com/mcg)

The above research by McKinsey reveals that there is a looming crisis ahead globally due to shortage of skills among people. Previously we found shortage of jobs and more qualified candidates. However, currently we find more qualified candidates and less competent candidates with skill set, tool set and mindset to grab employability opportunities. We find the problem is acute among Indian students who pass out from educational institutions with qualifications, not with competencies. It is known as unemployability which is different from unemployment. Unemployabliity is about having employment opportunities but the candidates do not have the requisite skills and abilities to grab them despite having academic qualifications. In contrast, unemployment is about having eligibility, suitability and capability but there are no employment opportunities. Therefore, Indian students must enhance their employment opportunities by develop requisite skills both in soft and hard skills to grow professionally.

Students must acquire non-academic skills and abilities that support academic qualifications to grab the employment opportunities. That means they must supplement their academic qualifications with a specific skill set, mindset and toolset which we can call soft skills. Students must acquire soft skills that enable them to equip with competencies that support their qualifications.

Connect Campus with Corporate

Here are the ways to bridge the gap of unemployability through integrated and holistic approach by various stakeholders including educational institutions, industry, educators, students, government and non-governmental organizations.

- It is disheartening to note that Indian education system is producing educated illiterates. It is here the collective role of all stakeholders such as faculty, recruiters, students and directors of educational institutions is imperative. There must be an integrated approach to handle unemployability in educational institutions. The educational institutions need to understand the requirements of the industry. At the same time, the industry needs to understand the limitations of the educational institutions. As soft skills are directly proportional to employability, there is need to customize the soft skills training programs as per the needs of the industry, not the other way round.
- Both academia and industry cannot operate in different orbits. They have to be within the same orbit leveraging their strengths for creating productive people. People often talk of interface between academia and industry.

However, it should be beyond interface and can be to the extent of wedding between the academia and the industry to create employable and enlightened professionals.

- The faculty must understand the needs of the students from time to time and evolve their teaching styles to suit the learning styles of students. It leads to right chemistry between the faculty and the students. It is not what you know matters but what you cater to the students ultimately matters.
- The academia must foresee the needs of the students through thorough research and prepare flexible curriculum with flexible learning styles to achieve the desired outcomes.
- Team teaching comes in handy to bridge the gap between the campus and the industry. In this method, both the educator and the industry expert undertake the teaching session while the educator places emphasis on the theory and the industry expert focuses on the application of the theoretical concepts. It helps students have the cake and eat it too as it paves relating the reel content with real life events.
- The academia is under theoretical perspective while the industrial world is under practical perspective. Both need to communicate, understand, empathize, and appreciate the compulsions and constraints and work in harmony to produce students who are industry compatible and employable.
- There is a strong need to develop human capital. No country can progress without the development of human capital. It is always the man behind the machine counts, not the machine behind the man. Both management and engineering institutions are the backbone of any country as they produce managers and engineers and collectively produce technocrats and leaders for the industry.
- The faculty should develop its own soft skills content as they know the real pulse of the students. They

should be exposed to the corporate establishments for understanding and appreciating their needs. It enables them to craft the content to suit as per the corporate expectations.

- Both faculty and students should be open and receptive for honing soft skills in order to survive and succeed in the corporate world. There must be consensus between the campus and the industry in developing and delivering the content about employability skills. It is necessary to blend soft and hard skills to produce successful engineers and managers right from the educational institutions.
- There must be drastic changes in the educational system that can connect educational institutions, students, faculty, recruiters and other non governmental bodies to ensure that India produces the employable youth.

To summarize, Indian students must understand the gaps in the present educational system and work towards developing the skills and abilities to back up their educational qualifications to enhance their employability and excel professionally.

> "If words of command are not clear and distinct, if orders are not thoroughly understood, the general is to blame. But if his orders are clear, and the soldiers nevertheless disobey, then it is the fault of their officers."
>
> *–Sun Tzu*

Remember: *Improve your skills constantly.*

REFERENCES

'Education to employment: Designing a system that works' by Mona Mourshed, Diana Farrell and Dominic Barton.

www.mckinsey.com/mcg

6

Do Your Duty

"The Bhagavad-Gita has a profound influence on the spirit of mankind by its devotion to God which is manifested by actions."

– Dr. Albert Schweitzer

Throughout my life, I followed Lord Sri Krishna's message to Arjun in *Bhagwad Gita*, "Action is thy duty, reward is not thy concern." The message conveys that you have a right to perform your prescribed duty, but you are not entitled to the fruits of action. Never consider yourself the cause of the results of your activities. The message helped me focus on my efforts rather than on constantly craving for outcome and concerned for not accomplishing them. When we often look at the results we tend to get demotivated and lose focus from our efforts especially when we don't achieve the expected outcome.

During my teaching and training programs I observed that the Genration Y is very smart and ambitious. They are highly competitive; good at technology; have quick thinking, and above all, possess high intelligence levels. However, I find them to be an impatient lot as they want to achieve success quickly and sometimes through shortcuts. If they don't achieve success, they quickly get upset. They often pose questions such as how to reach top positions quickly and to become CEO quickly. While I appreciate their enthusiasm to make it big in a huge way in the young age; and their intelligence; and unconventional approach, I advise them to be patient to achieve their goals. I share with them the Lord Sri Krishna's message. They probe me further, "What is the use of putting efforts when we don't get rewards?" I smile and explain them as follows:

The outcome of our efforts depends on several factors and we cannot predict them. There are a number of people who put their efforts to achieve success but lose focus as they don't get the expected results. If Edison lost focus, he wouldn't have invented a light bulb; if Alexander Graham Bell lost focus, he wouldn't have invented the telephone; if Colonel Sanders lost focus, he wouldn't have founded KFC. All these people worked hard continuously by finding out the ways and means to accomplish their goals. If they focused too much on rewards during their efforts they would have lost their focus quickly as they could not get the results quickly. Hence, youth must learn to be patient and contribute their best constantly to achieve their goals and objectives.

The outcome of our efforts depends on our patience, perseverance, timing, taking feedback regularly, and a little bit of God's grace. We can manage certain forces and factors which are in our hands, not the ones that are beyond our control. Hence, trust in God, do your best and I'm sure God will handhold you. Here are the tools for Gen Y to fast-track their careers:

Tools to Fast-track Your Career

- Stay focused on your goals clearly. Put efforts consistently and constantly and take feedback regularly.
- Be a self-starter, not a kick-starter. Take initiative and responsibility for your life and career.
- Be resourceful and work with what you have rather than blaming the people and circumstances around you. Remember, it is the bad tradesman who blames his tools.
- Capitalize on your strengths and guard from your weaknesses.
- Attend training programs to convert your knowledge into skills and to be competent in the workplace to excel professionally.
- Hire a coach or mentor in your area of interest and follow his/her guidance.
- Update yourself constantly. Remember that what worked for others might not work for you and what worked in the past might not work for you now as times and technologies are changing rapidly.

Follow these tools meticulously and work hard as per the message given by Lord Sri Krishna, and I am sure your outcome will chase you rather than your efforts chasing your outcome. Eulogizing on *Bhagwad Gita* Aldus Huxley said, "*The Gita* is one of the clearest and most comprehensive one, of the summaries and systematic spiritual statements of the perennial philosophy ever to have been done."

Your duty is only to act, not to hanker after the outcome. Your efforts will ensure positive outcome. But don't think too much on outcome as it takes its own time. When you strengthen your roots you get your fruits automatically. Hence, focus on strengthening your roots. God has bigger plans for you.

Keep working hard!

> "When doubts haunt me, when disappointments stare me in the face, and I see not one ray of hope on the horizon, I turn to *Bhagavad Gita* and find a verse to comfort me; and I immediately begin to smile in the midst of overwhelming sorrow. Those who meditate on *the Gita* will derive fresh joy and new meanings from it every day."
>
> – *Mahatma Gandhi*

Remember: *Fast-track your career.*

7

Hit Bull's Eye

"Your purpose explains what you are doing with your life. Your vision explains how you are living your purpose. Your goals enable you to realize your vision."

– Bob Proctor

Hitting the bull's eye sounds like hitting the centre of the target in archery. It also means accomplishing your goals accurately or achieving success in your life the way you wanted. When you want to hit the bull's eye you must believe in SMART goals where SMART is the acronym for specific, measurable, achievable, realistic, and time bound. That means when you set goals you have to be clear in your mind about your goals. You must find out how long it would take to accomplish them and whether they are achievable. Then you must ensure that your goal is realistic and time bound. Why do many set goals while only a few succeed in this world? It is because successful people stay focused clearly on their goals. There are people who set goals and put in half hearted efforts and fail finally. They change their goals as they failed to accomplish them. In fact, you must change your strategies to reach your goals, not your goals as confucius rightly put it, "When it is obvious that the goals cannot be reached, don't adjust the goals, adjust the action steps."

Advantages of Goal Setting

There are several advantages with goal setting. Goals remove negative thoughts from your mind. Our human mind gets approximately 55,000 thoughts in a day, and mostly we get negative thoughts. That is the reason most of the people get quickly attracted to negative things rather than positive things. Therefore, goals remove negative thoughts and replace with positive thoughts thus enhancing your attitude. Goals also help you stay focused. Focus is the key thing to succeed in this world. When you look at Steve Jobs he was an amazing example of focus on innovation. He dedicated his entire life on innovation and succeeded. Nothing distracted him. Hence, goals will enhance your focus. Goals will also manage your time. God gifted us with 24 hours. It is the gift all human beings equally got and we must know how to make use of it. Having goals will help us utilize our time and prioritize the tasks thus enhancing success. Goals help you to be resourceful as you utilize what you have rather than blaming circumstances.

Goals help enhance your longevity. If people don't have goals they reach saturation point quickly and find that there is no meaning to life. Viktor Frankl was a renowned psychiatrist who was a Jew. He was put in concentration camps during the Second World War by Hitler. He was a lean person and offered only bowl of soup to survive everyday. While his friends died in the concentration camp he survived despite being physically weak as he had a goal to author a book; and he authored one of the best books in the world—*Man's Search for Meaning*. Hence, goals will enhance your longevity and provide meaning to your life.

How to Hit the Bull's Eye?

> "Success can be defined as the progressive realization of a predetermined goal." – *John C. Maxwell*

Write down your goals as inking is more effective than thinking. Read your goals daily twice before you go to bed and after you wake from your bed. When you read before you go to bed the goals will go to your subconscious mind and sink effectively. If you go out of track your goals will remind you to be within the track.

Divide your goals into short-term and long-term goals. Make sure that your short-term goals are well aligned with your long-terms goals. Ensure that there are no contradictions between them. Ensure consistency and keep putting your efforts. During the journey, you will find lots of distractions. Anticipate the threats and keep moving forward. Sometimes you may encounter with external threats which are unknown. Hence, manage them and mould yourself as per the situation and make sure that you fall within the chosen track as and when you are pulled out of the tracks.

To accomplish your goals you need to take baby steps and divide your goal into small ones. You must take up little by little; execute the activities; and integrate them to accomplish them. As Rome was not built in a day, your regular and consistent efforts will take you hitting the bull's eye. Louis L'Amour rightly said, "Victory is won not in miles, but in inches. Win a little now, hold your ground, and later win a little more." For instance, when an author wants to write a book s/he conceives an idea and then does an intensive research to find out whether the book is unique and feasible to write. S/he keeps the profile of the audience in view; divides the tentative book into various chapters; and then writes each chapter. While making the book there will be many changes but the basic idea remains intact. When a director wants to make film s/he divides his or her entire movie into small pieces based on locations, availability of actors and proceeds making film. Finally, s/he integrates; fills the gaps wherever required; changes certain aspects during film-making; and finally makes the film. Similarly, when you want to accomplish your goals, you must set your goals based on your passion; divide them into short and long-term goals and work on them regularly.

When you look at most of the achievers they are persistent. They failed a number of times; learned lessons and moved forward with energy and enthusiasm. They demonstrated tremendous tenacity and resilience. Hence, keep moving forward towards your goals and hit the bull's eye by managing external threats and molding as per the situation to soar like an eagle.

Make Your Mark

Ask yourself how you would like to be remembered in your lifetime. Do you like to be remembered like Mahatma Gandhi or Mother Teresa or Martin Luther King? Do you like to be remembered like Alexander the Great or Napoleon Bonaparte? Do you like to be remembered like Abraham Lincoln or Barack Obama? Do you like to be remembered like Bill Gates or Steve Jobs? Whatever the way you want to be remembered, you must have a broad vision accordingly and work on it continuously with a passion to make it big. When others can achieve it why cannot you? The journey of thousand miles starts with the first step. Hence, take the first step to achieve whatever you want in your life and enjoy the journey by focusing firmly on your destination to hit the bull's eye.

All the best!

"If you can't fly, run!
If you can't run, walk!
If you can't walk, crawl!
But whatever you do, keep moving towards your goal..."

–Martin Luther King Jr.

Remember: *Set SMART goals.*

8

Change Your Mindset

"There is nothing training cannot do. Nothing is above its reach. It can turn bad morals to good; it can destroy bad principles and recreate good ones; it can lift men to angelship."

–Mark Twain

Is it possible to change the mindset of the people? If so, is changing the mindset of the people more challenging? What takes the people to change their mindset? Do people need counseling or inspiring trainers and teachers to change, or can they change by themselves? In fact, it is possible through all these ways. In addition, if the teachers and trainers are passionate; and are dedicated to make a difference in the lives of others with a true heart; it is possible to change their mindset. Here are my four experiences to share with you that help you change the way you think, and look at the issues in a new perspective to come out with flying colours.

My First Story

During my lifetime, I conducted a number of training programs and replied the queries of my audiences. At the end of the each session, I ask the audience to come out with questions to clarify them. I follow Kirkpatrick evaluation method to know how far the participants understood the essence, and are able to apply in their real lives. I ask the participants several questions and especially the following question: "What did you learn in my training program?" In my recent training program a participant responded with excitement, "Sir, you changed the way we think! You changed our mindsets! It's a great takeaway out of your training program." I was very much impressed with his response as I never got such responses from my audience in my previous training programs. Usually the participants explain what they learned from my training programs. However, it was a typical response from one of my participants. Hence, the response registered in my mind firmly. And since then I started to focus more on changing the mindset of the people apart from sharing my knowledge.

A teacher or trainer is effective when s/he delivers the content as per the expectations of the audiences. When the trainer gets such responses s/he gets motivated and becomes more passionate to share his/her knowledge. The trainer becomes more responsible to inspire participants.

My Second Story

A fan of mine often complained against his employer for not hiking his increment despite putting his best performance. There's a sycophant within his department who was close to his boss and carried wrong information against my fan. I counseled him to talk to his boss directly about his years of performance and contribution to the organization, and request for a raise. He told me that he'd tried but it was of no use. I counseled him to look elsewhere for better prospects where his talents will be recognized. He applied for openings and got better offer with higher designation and a hike of 50 percent in his salary. He thanked me for timely counseling because he never thought in that way. I felt happy that I changed his mindset and the way he looked at the problems rather than brooding over them.

My Third Story

A known person who was older to me in age rushed to my cabin when I was busy browsing the computer and said, "Sir, my job is in danger as we didn't get the requisite number of students to join the educational institution." Even I was aware of the looming threat but I kept cool and concentrated on my research in leadership. I recognized from her body language that she wanted a positive and consoling response from me. I asked her, "Is your CV strong?" She pondered a moment and said, "Yes, there's no problem with my CV and boasted about her academic achievements." She radiated confidence. I reminded her, what Lord Shri Krishna told to Arjun in *Bhagwat Gita*, "Action is thy duty; reward is not thy concern" which means "do your duty and don't look for rewards". She was confused for a moment with my sermon as she never expected such kind of response from me. I explained her in a simple language as follows: "Go to your cabin and do your work sincerely and God will take care of you." She understood my message well and left the room thanking me. I felt happy that I allayed her apprehensions and changed her mindset to focus on work rather than worrying about her job security.

My Fourth Story

One day I met my neighbor who passed out of the college 5 months ago. I enquired him about the status of his employment search. He said that he had been trying for the last 5 months and added that he got an employment offer from a call centre (BPO) to work but he refused to work. I asked him, "What is the problem? He said, "The employer wanted me to sign an agreement for a year to work, and I didn't join as it might prevent me from pursuing other prospects." I enquired him, "Is it the only problem or are there any other reasons for being unemployed?" He asserted, "That is the only problem." I enquired, "When did you get the employment offer." He replied, "5 months ago." I probed further, "What're doing now?" He replied, "I am still searching for employment." I counseled him as follows: "You've already spent 5 months without any employment. You should have joined the call centre (BPO). They provide you free accent training and you would have improved your communication skills. Nowadays there's unemployment problem. Whatever the offer you get you must accept and work there for some time. You develop connections; build your confidence; get exposed to the outside world; gain experience; and generate income for your family."

He appreciated my advice and said, "Sir, I never thought the way you thought. Thanks for your suggestion. I'll go for employment and then see the possibilities in compatible with my qualifications, competencies and tastes." I was happy as he took my advice positively and changed his mindset.

From these four stories, it is obvious that everybody knows everything but how many of us follow them properly. Anybody can teach and train but it takes tons of passion and efforts to change the mindset of the audience and the people around you. Precisely, it requires a lot of passion on the part of the trainer or teacher to change the mindset of the people. Hence, change the people the way they think so that they will feel confident and address the challenges unconventionally and express their gratitude to you forever.

"Those that won't be counseled can't be helped."

–Benjamin Franklin

***Remember:** Change the way you think.*

9

Cross the Thin Line

"It's a thin line between insanity and genius"

– Oscar Levant

In my recent leadership training program, one of the participants asked me the styles of leadership and which leadership style would be the best. I replied that there is no specific leadership style that works permanently as leaders have to mould as per the people, tasks and the prevailing situation. Above all, they must stick to their convictions and adopt the style that demands as per the situation. I said that there were a number of leadership styles such as autocratic, democratic, delegative, transformational, transactional and situational. He further probed what type of leadership style both Alexander the Great and Adolph Hitler adopted. I replied him that both were autocratic leaders. He further probed why Hitler earned bad name while Alexander earned good name. I clarified his question as follows:

Although both Alexander and Adolph Hitler were autocratic leaders, Alexander didn't go against any community. He wanted to conquer the world and with tons of difficulties and challenges, he conquered finally. Hence, he was considered to be the Great. In contrast, Hitler went against Jews and put them in concentration camps and brought them misery. It is often the thin line that separates good and bad leadership. So is the case of Alexander and Hitler as the former crossed the thin line while the latter failed to cross it and failed miserably finally.

There is always a thin line that separates success and failure. Although Steve Jobs was an autocratic leader he succeeded as a leader and proved as a better business leader than Steve Ballmer of Microsoft as the former crossed the thin line. It is the thin line that separates good person and bad person. In the Hindu epic, *Ramayan*, although Ravan was a demon king he was a great ruler. In the epic, *Mahabharat*, although Duryodhan was a villain to Pandavas he was a great ruler and a great friend to Karn. They failed as leaders because they failed to cross the thin line.

It is the thin line that separates professionalism and unprofessionalism. It is the thin line that separates ethics and fraud. When you look at Ramalinga Raju of former Satyam Computers, he failed and came below the thin line. When you look at Rajat Gupta, former director of Goldman Sachs he failed and came below the thin line. He was sentenced for 2 year jail term and fine of $5 million for leaking confidential board-room information. Hence, leaders must be careful from this judgment and learn lessons to avoid such things because people have lots of expectations on leaders at the top level. Leaders must remember that if they lose money they lose nothing but if they lose their character and trust, they lose everything that they made during their lifetimes. Publilius Syrus rightly quoted, "What is left when honor is lost?"

B.C. Forbes remarked, "We cannot hold a torch to light another's path without brightening our own." As a leader, if you do ten things, and of which, nine are good things while one is bad, people remember one bad thing rather than the nine good things you have done. Although people are not perfect they expect their leaders to be perfect and role models. Hence, as a leader you have a huge responsibility to set an example to others to have everlasting impact on your followers. Don't get tempted by short-terms results. In contrast, look for long-term impact although it takes a very long time. Learn to understand what the thin line is, and strive to cross the thin line to achieve all-round success and to leave a mark behind for others to follow.

Remember that no person is entirely good; and no person is entirely bad. Every bad person has a great virtue and every good person has a bad quality. Life is a game! The people who know the rules of the game and follow the rules meticulously become successful and those who fail to follow become unsuccessful. Identify the thin line, cross it, and grow accordingly. Remember the sage words of Benjamin Disraeli, "Life is too short to be little." It is your life! There is only one life! Hence, do what you feel good and for the prosperity of the people around you to excel as a great leader. All the best!

> "When in doubt, make a fool of yourself. There is a microscopically thin line between being brilliantly creative and acting like the most gigantic idiot on earth. So, what the hell, leap."
>
> – *Cynthia Heimel*

Remember: *Identify the thin line.*

10

Emphasize on Achievements, not Affiliations

"It is all one to me if a man comes from Sing Sing or Harvard. We hire a man, not his history."

– Henry Ford

I have seen a senior faculty member who often toots her own horns about her educational background as she acquired qualifications from prestigious educational institutions. She ridicules another faculty member who acquired qualifications from low profile educational institutions. I started to think on this, and explored to write an article weighing both pros and cons. Are affiliations more important than achievements? Are the people qualified from prestigious educational institutions more competent than the ones from ordinary educational institutions? Are the candidates qualified from ordinary educational institutions less knowledgeable than the ones from extraordinary educational institutions?

It is indeed tough to conclude that the people qualified from prestigious educational institutions are smarter than the ones from low-profile educational institutions. It appears like an MBA degree holder from a prestigious institution can excel as a better CEO than the one from low-profile institution.

When we look at Bill Gates, Steve Jobs, Michael Dell, Mark Zuckerberg, and Larry Ellison, they are college dropouts but proved themselves as successful CEOs. When you look at the 16th President of America, Abraham Lincoln, he was a self-educated man who proved far better than 43rd President of America, George W. Bush who earned his MBA from Harvard Business School. Hence, it is unfair to jump to conclusion that the people from prestigious institutions are always better material than the ones from ordinary institutions. However, people from prestigious institutions have several advantages. They are equipped with employability skills, and companies prefer to hire them based on the educational and institutional affiliation. They enjoy amazing ambience; have better visibility; and grow their career ladder quickly due to their connections created from the classroom. The knowledge they share is qualitative and the amount of efforts they put in are smarter thus paying rich dividends. On the other hand, the people from ordinary institutions put a lot of hard work as they have to slog hard for acquiring knowledge and connecting with the right people. They go by stairs as they are not equipped to go by elevator unlike the people from extraordinary institutions. Hence, it all depends on the individuals, not institutions; and achievements, not affiliations.

People from prestigious institutions often remain in their comfort zones while the people from ordinary institutions remain in their effective zones to prove themselves. There are instances where the people qualified from prestigious institutions come up with high egos and become too big for their shoes, and finally falling flat on the ground. In contrast, the people who come from grass root level understand the value of life and empathize with others. They take baby steps and grow steadily and consistently and rarely do they look back as their failure rate is lower.

Ordinary versus Extraordinary Educational Institutions

Anyone can join ordinary educational institutions by fulfilling the basic requirements and following guidelines despite not being good academically and sound financially. However, only the cream joins extraordinary educational institutions. Self starters join ordinary institutions and kick starters join extraordinary institutions. The admissions into ordinary institutions are flexible while the admissions into extraordinary institutions are strict. There is often spoon-feeding in ordinary institutions while there is self-feeding in extraordinary institutions. The teaching pedagogy in ordinary institutions is traditional and examination-oriented while the teaching pedagogy in extraordinary institutions is updated and innovative. The extraordinary institutions adopt team-based, case-study driven, and out-of-the-box approach leading to many solutions to problems. The students are reshuffled physically in the classroom and it creates new vibes and ideas. They understand the psychology of other students and think critically, analytically and logically; acquire and apply knowledge effectively apart from building great connections. In addition, they are connected with other bright students virtually thus sharing and broadening their knowledge greatly. Above all, the faculty in ordinary institutions serves as resource persons while the faculty in extraordinary institutions serves as moderators thus adding value to the existing cream.

The X-Factor Makes the Difference

The X-factor counts more than anything else. American President, Abraham Lincoln finished only one year of formal schooling. Andrew Jackson excelled without formal education. Andrew Carnegie, industrialist; and Frederick Henry Royce, co-founder of Rolls-Royce are elementary school dropouts. Richard Branson of Virgin Group; Ray Kroc of McDonald, Walt Disney of Walt Disney Company; and Amadeo Peter Giannini, founder of Bank of America are high school dropouts. James Cameron, Oscar-winning director, Larry Ellison, co-founder of Oracle and Michael Dell, founder of Dell Computers are college dropouts. Benjamin Franklin, inventor, author, entrepreneur; Christopher Columbus, explorer, and Thomas Edison, inventor of the light bulb are home-schooled. Hence, you can draw inspiration from such great achievers who reached the tipping point despite lack of adequate education due to their X-factor.

Bad with Books but Good with Hands

Lao Tzu quoted, "Those who have knowledge, don't predict. Those who predict, don't have knowledge." There are people who are bad with books but good with hands became job providers and leaders. At the same time, there are people who are good with books but bad with hands became job seekers and remained as followers. Hence, it is tough to come to conclusion that the people who are qualified from prestigious institutions achieve amazingly. But it can be firmly summed up that their success rate will be higher.

God gifted unique talents to everyone. However, all are not blessed with resources to pursue their education in prestigious institutions. Hence, we cannot underestimate the people acquiring qualifications from ordinary educational institutions. What counts at the end of the day is how you acquire and apply your knowledge; how you deliver your goods; and above all, the difference you make in the lives of others. To conclude, it is the achievements count, not affiliations; it is the individuals count, not institutions.

> "The difference between a successful person and others is not a lack of strength, not a lack of knowledge, but rather in a lack of will."
>
> – *Vincent T. Lombardi*

***Remember:** Be good with your hands.*

REFERENCE

http://www.youngentrepreneur.com/blog/100-top-entrepreneurs-who-succeeded-without-a-college-degree/

11

Excel as an Entrepreneur

"I wanted to be an editor or a journalist, I wasn't really interested in being an entrepreneur, but I soon found I had to become an entrepreneur in order to keep my magazine going."

– Richard Branson

Recently I was invited for a workshop on Entrepreneurial Development Program. The presenter explained the importance of entrepreneurship and how to start a business and the challenges involved in setting up an enterprise. He said that he had his own business and was working as a consultant for several companies on setting up enterprises. He shared the challenges he encountered initially when he set up his own small business as there was resistance from his parents. He showed video clipping of a few successful entrepreneurs who started from nowhere and reached the pinnacle of their entrepreneurial journey. It was inspiring session with full of entrepreneurial ideas and insights. I decided to explore this topic further for the benefit of my students and those who have myths about entrepreneurship and are passionate about it.

There is no doubt that Indians have the entrepreneurial mindset and most of the students want to become job providers rather than job seekers. However, most of the parents don't encourage their children to set up businesses as there are more challenges involved in it. In case of failure, nobody comes forward to support. There is no governmental support. There are no social security measures. In case of bankruptcy, the law takes its own time to clear the cases. There is a social stigma attached to failures in India. Likewise, there are a number of reasons why Indian parents don't encourage their children to pursue their entrepreneurial journey. They encourage their children to play safe and advise them to become job seekers. Since most of the parents are in middle and old age, they want their old age to be secured without any financial hiccups. They have apprehensions what would happen to them in their old age if their children fail in business.

Job Seeker versus Job Provider

> "You need to set up long-term goals... You can then go on to achieving the short-term objectives. If you go headlong into the short-term without planning for the long term, it won't happen." – *Mr M.V. Kamath, CEO of ICICI Bank*

If you are a money-driven, become a job seeker. In contrast, if you are a value-driven, become a job provider. If you have the mindset of 'accumulation', become a job seeker. In contrast, if you have the mindset of 'contribution', become a job provider. If you brood over the problems, become a job seeker. In contrast, if you find solutions for the problems, become a job provider. If you think inside the box, become a job seeker. In contrast, if you think outside the box, become a job provider. If you want to survive like any other ordinary person, become a job seeker. In contrast, if you want to succeed like an extraordinary person, become a job provider. If you want to get into rat race, become a job seeker. In contrast, if you want to stand out and be a trailblazer, become a job provider.

Challenges for Entrepreneurs

The students must remember that it is not easy to set up their own businesses. There are many challenges involved in it. They have to encounter several challenges from beginning to the end. They must know how to convert threats into opportunities. They must learn to see the door that is opened rather than the one that is closed. Michael Gerber rightly remarked, "The entrepreneur in us sees opportunities everywhere we look, but many people see only problems everywhere they look. The entrepreneur in us is more concerned with discriminating between opportunities than he or she is with failing to see the opportunities." They have to work round the clock. They must arrange capital. They must face cut-throat competition. They cannot predict what happens next resulting in high stress levels. Most of the threats arise from external business environment. However, they can face all these challenges easily if they are passionate about entrepreneurship. They must understand that entrepreneurship is not for fainthearted, but for brave hearted.

Risks in Entrepreneurship

Students must learn that whatever the business decisions they make might not result in success as some of them are bound to fail. They must also understand that success rate for an entrepreneur is low. Brian Tracy, in *The Psychology of Achievement* (2002), talks about four millionaires who made their fortunes by the age of 35. They were involved in an average of 17 businesses before finding the one that took them to the top. They kept trying and changing until they found something that worked for them. If they have passion for entrepreneurship, and are willing to take risk and learn lessons and move forward with tenacity and resilience, then entrepreneurship is the right option. They must learn that there is an element of risk in jobs also as there is no guarantee in getting the employment and ensuring its longevity even after employed as employees can be fired at any time. They must understand that there is risk involved in being a job seeker and job provider. Above all, they must overcome from the fear of failures and criticism to succeed as entrepreneurs.

If Dirubhai Ambani remained as an employee as petrol pump attendant, would he have set up Reliance Empire? If Narayana Murthy remained in Patni Computers as an employee, would he have founded Infosys Technology Ltd? Hence, remove your mental limitations; and take risks to excel as successful entrepreneurs. Debunk the myth that Indians work for others, not for themselves. If Indians work for themselves by setting up enterprises imagine the amount of wealth we would create for India and the type of India we would live in. To sum up, if India has to grow as a strong economy and a global super power, we need more of job providers rather than job seekers.

> "Entrepreneurs are risk takers, willing to roll the dice with their money or reputation on the line in support of an idea or enterprise. They willingly assume responsibility for the success or failure of a venture and are answerable for all its facets."
>
> – *Victor Kiam*

Remember: *Become a job provider.*

12

Explore Entrepreneurial Opportunities

"The purpose of a business is to create a customer."

– Peter Drucker

There are a number of people who have zeal and enthusiasm to excel as entrepreneurs. But they are not encouraged in India due to number of reasons. In addition, they have a myth that entrepreneurs are extraordinary individuals. But the fact is that entrepreneurs are the ordinary individuals with extraordinary business acumen. They observe a lot and identify solutions for the problems. When ordinary people brood over the problems they think about the prospects. They know how to convert threats into opportunities. If you want to excel as an entrepreneur you must identify the problems around you and address them with solutions. Here are a few the opportunities for aspiring entrepreneurs:

Entrepreneurial Opportunities

"Structure your selling process so that each state either answers a question or solves a problem of the customer."

– Brian Tracy

India has a number of challenges. Identify the challenges and address them. For instance, we have an unorganized retail sector. Think of organizing it effectively. We have bad roads leading to many accidents. Think of infrastructure development. We have traffic problems. Think of constructing flyovers and streamlining them. There is heavy traffic jams in trains and buses. Think of alternative mode of transportation. There are a lot of Indians all over the world working and they need to travel by air. Think of building international airports and provide cost-effective air services. We have housing problem. Think of constructing houses at low cost. We are successful in manufacturing 'Nano' car, we can think similarly in building low-cost houses for poor people.

Remember the cliché: below average individuals think about individuals, average individuals think about issues and above average individuals think about ideas. Therefore, if you want to excel as an entrepreneur look at the issues and explore ideas that can be conceptualized and made viable and feasible.

Entrepreneurs Excelled without Education

There are leaders who excelled without adequate education. There are leaders who left their indelible mark without college, high school, and elementary education. And some made it big through home-schooling. Let us look at some of the leaders:

American President, Abraham Lincoln finished only one year of formal schooling. Another American president, Andrew Jackson excelled without formal education.

Elementary School Dropouts: Andrew Carnegie, industrialist and philanthropist; Frederick Henry Royce, auto designer, multimillionaire co-founder of Rolls-Royce; Isaac Merrit Singer, sewing machine inventor, founder of Singer; and Marcus Loew, multimillionaire founder of Loews theaters, co-founder of MGM movie studio are elementary school dropouts.

High School Dropouts: Richard Branson of Virgin Group; Ray Kroc of McDonald, Walt Disney of Walt Disney Company; Amadeo Peter Giannini, multimillionaire founder of Bank of America; Anne Beiler, multimillionaire co-founder of Auntie Anne's Pretzels; Ansel Adams, world-famous photographer; Ashley Qualls, founder of Whateverlife.com; Barbara Lynch, chef, owner of a group of restaurants, worth over $10 million, in Boston; Bob Proctor, motivational speaker, bestselling author, and co-founder of Life Success Publishing; Carl Lindner, billionaire investor, founder of United Dairy Farmers; Charles Culpeper, owner and CEO of Coca Cola; Dave Thomas, billionaire founder of Wendy's; Dov Charney, founder of American Apparel; Frederick "Freddy" Laker, billionaire airline entrepreneur; George Eastman, multimillionaire inventor, Kodak founder; Henry J. Kaiser, multimillionaire and founder of Kaiser Aluminum; Hyman Golden, co-founder of Snapple; Simon Cowell, TV producer, music judge, American Idol, The X Factor, and Britain's Got Talent; Tom Anderson, co-founder and "friend" of MySpace; Vidal Sassoon, founder of Vidal Sassoon, multimillionaire; W.T. Grant, founder of W.T. Grant department stores, multimillionaire; and Wally "Famous" Amos, multimillionaire entrepreneur, author, talent agent, founder of Famous Amos cookies.

College Dropouts: Ben Kaufman, 21-year-old serial entrepreneur, founder of Kluster; Craig McCaw, billionaire founder of McCaw Cellular; David Geffen, billionaire founder of Geffen Records and co-founder of DreamWorks; David Neeleman, founder of JetBlue airlines; David Ogilvy, advertising executive and copywriter; David Oreck, multimillionaire founder of The Oreck Corporation; DeWitt Wallace, founder and publisher of Reader's Digest; Jack Crawford Taylor, founder of Enterprise Rent-a-Car; Jake Nickell, co-founder and CEO of Threadless.com; James Cameron, Oscar-winning director, screenwriter, and producer; Larry Ellison, billionaire co-founder of Oracle software company; Mark Ecko, founder of Mark Ecko Enterprises; Mary Kay Ash, founder of Mary Kay Inc; Michael Dell, billionaire founder of Dell Computers, which started out of his college dorm room; Michael Rubin, founder of Global Sports; Ray Kroc, founder of McDonald's; Richard Branson, billionaire founder of Virgin Records, Virgin Atlantic Airways, Virgin Mobile; Ron Popeil, multimillionaire founder of Ronco, inventor, producer, infomercial star; Rush Limbaugh, multi-millionaire media mogul, radio talk show host; Russell Simmons, co-founder of Def Jam records, founder of Russell

Simmons Music Group, Phat Farm fashions, bestselling author; Sean John Combs, entertainer, producer, fashion designer, and entrepreneur; Shawn Fanning, developer of Napster; Steve Madden, shoe designer; Steve Wozniak, co-founder of Apple, billionaire; Ted Murphy, founder of social media company Izea Entertainment; Theodore Waitt, billionaire founder of Gateway Computers; and Ty Warner, billionaire developer of Beanie Babies, real estate investor, and hotel owner are college dropouts.

Home-Schooled: Benjamin Franklin, inventor, scientist, author, entrepreneur; Christopher Columbus, explorer, discoverer of new lands; David Karp, founder of Tumblr dropped out of school at 15, then homeschooled; Thomas Edison, inventor of the light bulb, and phonograph are home-schooled.

Hence, you can draw inspiration from these great achievers who reached the tipping point despite lack of adequate education due to their X-factor and entrepreneurial zeal and enthusiasm.

Go for Entrepreneurship!

Identify the needs, expectations and aspirations of the people around you and come out with viable and feasible solutions through an entrepreneurial blueprint. In addition, find out the fast changing needs, tastes and temperaments of the consumers and provide goods and services accordingly. Steve Jobs was successful as an entrepreneur as he was passionate and innovated constantly as per the customers' expectations and aspirations. He rightly remarked, "You can't just ask customers what they want and then try to give that to them. By the time you get it built, they'll want something new."

People often think ill of money, but we cannot survive without money. Money is needed to ensure comfortable living. Hence, develop a healthy attitude towards money to create more wealth for the betterment of society. Remember that entrepreneurship is not for fainthearted but for strong hearted. Entrepreneurship is not a cakewalk but walking a tightrope beset with challenges round the clock. Are you ready? If yes, go for it!

> "If you want to build a sustainable business, then all your key stakeholders must believe that you are in it for the long-term."
>
> *– Mr S. Ramadorai, former CEO, TCS*

Remember: *Identify entrepreneurial opportunities.*

REFERENCE

http://www.youngentrepreneur.com/blog/100-top-entrepreneurs-who-succeeded-without-a-college-degree/

13

Apply 80/20 Principle to Achieve Excellence

"Whatever your present situation, I assure you that you are not your habits. You can replace old patterns of self-defeating behavior with new patterns, new habits of the effectiveness, happiness, and trust-based relationships."

– Stephen Covey

The 80:20 Principle is an interesting one and if you know how to apply it in your real life you can reap rewards tremendously. It is used in many areas including time management, marketing, performance, and leadership. It explains that if you identify 80 percent where your energies and efforts are wasted and focus on it effectively you can achieve success quickly. In other words, the principle asserts that approximately 80% of the effects come from 20% of the causes. It is known as Pareto Principle and also known as the law of the vital few. It sounds like quantity versus quality. Do you focus on quantity or quality? Do you focus on 80 waste and 20 utility? Do you focus on negativity or positivity? If you focus on quality, positivity, and 20 per cent utility then you can easily achieve whatever you want in your life.

It was Italian economist Vilfredo Pareto who stated that 80 percent of the land in Italy was owned by 20 percent people in 1906 based on his observation. Initially the concept was confined to economics and gradually it has been spread to other spheres. Although many people are aware of this principle a very few understand its application. In fact, application of principle is more important than acquisition of the principle as it helps to reap great rewards.

There are teachers who teach for long hours to students but there will not be any takeaways to the students. In contrast, there are teachers who teach for a limited hours but make a huge impact on the minds of students. Similarly, students must learn that how many hours they read is not important but how much knowledge they acquired is more important within a stipulated time. To go further, how much they applied in their real lives is more important than how much knowledge they acquired.

Emphasize on 20 and Eliminate 80

"Professionalism means consistency of quality."

– *Frank Tyger*

You can apply the 80/20 Rule in most of the areas provided you know the concept clearly. And when you apply it effectively you enjoy the difference you make in your life. To achieve quick success adopt the following tips:

- Focus on what you want, not what you don't want.
- Reflect and review periodically to stay focused and productive.
- Understand your priorities and focus on the precious ones that are close to your heart and you enjoy immensely.
- Change your mindset and focus on the ones that are close to your heart.

We meet many people in our lives but we enjoy a few of them as they make deep impact on us. You cannot do everything in life. Hence, separate the wheat from the chaff by focusing on your core talents and skills to achieve success quickly. Peter F. Drucker once said, "Efficiency is doing things right; effectiveness is doing the right things." Hence, be effective rather than efficient. In addition, efficiency is the foundation for survival and effectiveness is the foundation for success. How long you are into the race doesn't count but how you entered into the race counts. How much you learnt is not important but how much knowledge you shared with others is important. How much money you made is not important but how much difference you made in the lives of others count. Follow these timeless tools and principles and I am sure you find meaning in your life.

> "Men acquire a particular quality by constantly acting in a particular way."
>
> – *Aristotle*

Remember: *Emphasize quality, not quantity.*

14

Acquire Soft Skills

"In today's competitive environment, it is not enough to be the best in your field, intellectually. Competency is only half of what you need to climb the ladder of success. The other half is the softer side of you – it's that part of you that will be liked, admired, trusted and remembered."

– Carole Nicola Ides

Soft skills are essential irrespective of the level of management – low, middle and top level management. People rise in organizations due to hard skills but fall due to lack of soft skills. Senior executives need more of soft skills rather than hard skills. CEOs require more of soft skills rather than any other skills. Do the statements sound strange to you? Here is the answer:

According to the psychologist Daniel Goleman, soft skills are a combination of competencies that contribute to a person's ability to manage himself and relate to other people. These are the skills, abilities, and traits about the personality, attitude, and behavior of a person. They are the human skills that make a huge difference for your professional success. They are needed for good leaders to become great leaders. In contrast, hard skills are about your technical competence and domain expertise. Sometimes soft skills are equated with teamwork while hard skills with execution. Hence, executives must proportionately blend the soft and hard skills with leadership to excel as successful leaders. However, as they gain more experience they need more of soft skills because they work less on their hard skills and more on interpersonal skills. They are mostly into visioning, troubleshooting, and managing several stakeholders which demands soft skills and leadership skills.

Soft Skills for CEOs

CEOs must demonstrate both soft and hard skills with more emphasis on soft skills as they have to handle people. Dr. John Fleenor of the Center for Creative Leadership explains that the CEO's "soft" skills make all the difference. They must be good listeners, consensus builders, team players and empathizers. Hence, to grow the corporate ladder quickly, it is essential for executives to possess more of soft skills and less of hard skills. We can compare soft skills with emotional intelligence quotient (EQ) and hard skills with intelligence quotient (IQ). Succinctly, soft skills are twice as important as IQ or technical skills for the success of senior executives. Studies have shown that individuals with high emotional quotient are highly appreciated in the workplace and they tend to grow rapidly in the corporate ladder. Denis Waitley rightly quoted, "The winner's edge is not in a gifted birth, a high IQ, or in talent. The winner's edge is all in the attitude, not aptitude. Attitude is the criterion for success."

Ram Charan outlines the importance of both business acumen and people acumen for leaders in his book, *Leaders At All Levels*. He says, "Anyone can improve his or her ability to select and develop people's talents, but other aspects of people acumen are hard to teach. Leaders with people acumen have good instincts to anticipate problems among individuals who must work together, and to get them resolved. When leaders are unable to make good decisions, or any decisions at all, it may be that their business acumen is not expanding. They cannot be considered to have CEO potential." Here business acumen is equated with hard skills and people acumen with soft skills. We can also say that hard skills include IQ and soft skills include EQ.

EQ and Soft Skills

There are a number of definitions on emotional intelligence. For instance, Salovey and Mayer defined emotional intelligence in *Emotional Intelligence* as follows: "We define emotional intelligence as the subset of social intelligence that involves the ability to monitor one's own and others' feelings and emotions, to discriminate among them and to use this information to guide one's thinking and actions." And David Caruso goes further on it as follows: "It is very important to understand that emotional intelligence is not the opposite of intelligence, it is not the triumph of heart over head — it is the unique intersection of both." But I would like to define EQ as follows: "Emotional intelligence quotient is a five-step process of discovering your emotions; managing your emotions; motivating your emotions; discovering the emotions of the people around you, and managing their emotions to achieve organizational goals and objectives." Here people find it quite comfortable to discover, manage, and motivate, their emotions but they find it tough to discover the emotions of others and channel their emotions effectively. Hence, acquiring EQ is easier said than done. Although most of the people are aware of the definition of EQ they fail to apply and excel as leaders because managing the emotions of others is a highly challenging task and it consumes a lot of mental energies to set the things straight from time to time.

Soft Skills at all Levels

Entry level executives need both soft and hard skills to start with. As they attain experience they must acquire more of soft and conceptual skills as hard skills matter less. There are leaders who excelled as great leaders despite not being good at hard skills in a specific area as they are good at soft skills and converted soft skills into hard skills.

Employees must know how to gel well with others to minimize workplace conflicts and create a conducive climate to enhance organizational excellence and effectiveness. If employees don't possess soft skills a lot of time will be spent in firefighting thus deviating from the destined goals. Hence, soft skills are imperative for employees and more so for the senior executives to handle employees effectively. Especially in the prevailing tough times soft skills help retain the customers as the customers demand more from companies currently. Handling them with soft skills makes a huge difference in winning, and retaining them for a longer time.

While leading the employees, the leaders must learn that they are managing the emotions of their employees. And to manage the emotions of the employees, there is a need for soft skills rather than hard skills. Hard skills are essential to manage machine while soft skills are essential to lead men. Hence, in order to lead men, and to mange machine, material, and money it is essential to blend soft and hard skills proportionately to achieve the expected outcomes.

Soft Skills Fast-track Your Career Success

If you want to reach senior positions quickly in the corporate world you must emphasize more on EQ. And Mayer and Salovey rightly quoted, "People high in emotional intelligence are expected to progress more quickly through the abilities designated and to master more of them." In addition, research reveals that to reach the CEO position quickly executives must possess more of soft skills and emotional quotient. However strong in IQ and great experience they have, the executives must possess more EQ and great attitude to survive and inspire others to perform well. There are senior executives who fell flat on the ground despite being good at experience and IQ as they developed rotten attitude and became too big for their shoes due to high ego that arose from their strong hard skills. Hence, soft skills are essential for leaders to survive, succeed and to inspire others to enhance organizational excellence and effectiveness.

> "If words of command are not clear and distinct, if orders are not thoroughly understood, the general is to blame. But if his orders are clear, and the soldiers nevertheless disobey, then it is the fault of their officers."
>
> – *Sun Tzu*

Remember: *Blend your hard skills with soft skills.*

15

Learn NLP

"Organizations in the future will manage feelings, beliefs, perceptions and values—the asset of emotional capital—as the hidden resources with the power to translate people's knowledge into positive action."

– Kevin Thomson, author Emotional Capital

I led a webinar titled, "21 Success Sutras for Leaders" organized by Time Group in India. It was based on my authored book published by Pearson Education. At the end of the webinar, participants raised many questions on leadership and there was one question on the merits of NLP. I felt that there is enormous significance attached to NLP. Hence, I explored this concept and we will discuss about it briefly in this chapter.

What is NLP?

NLP is the acronym for Neuro-Linguistic Programming. It was coined by Richard Bandler, John Grinder and others in 1970s. It is a combination of three elements 'Neuro', 'Linguistic' and 'Programme'. The element 'Neuro' refers to the thinking patterns that make up the mental aspect of our strategies; the element 'Linguistic' refers to the way we use language both inwardly to ourselves (our 'inner dialogue') and outwardly in conversation with others; and the element 'Programme' refers to the way we run our strategies for getting results in all areas of life and work. It works on the premise that although you cannot change the world you can change the way in which you represent the world in your thinking. It is helpful as a teaching and learning tool. It helps you achieve excellence. It helps in personality development, improves communication skills and brings out behavioral changes to achieve all-round success in your life. Here are some more advantages in detail:

Advantages

NLP helps you discover your potential and passion. It leverages your unconscious mind and aligns both conscious and unconscious mind effectively. It helps you manage yourself and moulds you as per the external environment effectively. It differentiates between beliefs and facts, and you will realize that beliefs are not facts and appreciate that beliefs are emotionally held opinions that we take to be true and that determine our subsequent actions. It quickens your career growth and helps you grow professionally. It adjusts your inner dialogue as per the people around you to develop compatibility. You will be able to inspire others and you appreciate that there is no failure, only feedback.

In addition, NLP helps you become the way you want to become. It changes your mindset. It helps you achieve excellence by bridging the gap between what you don't have and what you want to have. It helps in your attitude building and empathizing with others. You look at the world differently and from others' perspective. It helps you find out your weaknesses and strengths and guard you from your weaknesses. It brings you awareness that people think differently and how to align and adjust your thinking with others' thinking and vice versa. It is rightly said that a battle is won twice — first in your mind and then in real life. Hence, it bridges the gap between your vision and execution to accomplish your goals.

It is not possible to change everything around us. Life is full of lessons and we must learn lessons and bridge both internal and external environment and mould ourselves accordingly to lead happily and successfully in this world. In this way, you become a manager of various aspects. If you succeed further you can excel as a leader to bring about the changes in others effectively. To conclude, what you think is what you get is the bottom line of NLP.

> "To change ourselves effectively, we first had to change our perceptions."
>
> – Stephen R. Covey, *The 7 Habits of Highly Effective People*

NLP Assessment

Here is a way to check what is true for you at each of these levels.

Consider the following questions for each level:

1. What is your overall purpose in life? What benefits do you seek to bring to others? (**Purpose**)
2. What kind of person are you, and how does this support the achievement of your overall purpose?(**Identity**)
3. What is important to you, and how does this support the kind of person you are? (**Values**)
4. How does what you believe support the achievement of what is important to you? (**Beliefs**)
5. What are your core talents, and how are you using them to achieve what is important to you? (**Capabilities**)
6. How is what you do (as a job and the way you behave moment by moment) an expression of who you truly are? (**Behavior**)
7. How is your environment an expression of who you are, and how are the people around you supporting you in what you want? (**Environment**)

If all these elements of yourself are pointing in the same direction, then you are congruent i.e. everything about you says the same thing. This is a very influential state to have. The reactions that you get will be feedback to who you truly are.

***Remember:** Mould yourself as per the situation.*

REFERENCE

Introducing NLP Sue Knight, Universities Press

16

Ask Right Questions

"To be able to ask a question clearly is two-thirds of the way to getting it answered."

– John Ruskin

Recently a prestigious international magazine sent me an invitation to feature my photo on its cover page. The editor wanted to publish my interview inside the magazine and sent me a set of questions for my response. I received the following questions:

How would you define leadership?

What's the difference between management and leadership?

To what extent are leaders born or made?

What are the key leadership challenges in modern organisations?

What is emerging as the key leadership model for the next decade?

How can individual managers develop their leadership capabilities?

What does current research say that helps us understand organizational leadership?

What kind of leadership is appropriate for the speed and complexity of change that we face now?

What leadership attributes are required with globalization?

How do we develop the next generation of leaders?

I was very much impressed with the pattern and framing of questions as it contained open-ended questions and started with easy questions first followed by thought provoking questions. I needed more time to respond as it needed an in-depth thinking and I want to deliver my best. I thought for a moment at the editor's intelligence to create questions and appreciated the editor for sending me interesting questions.

Questioning is an art and very few people are aware of it. Most of the students in the classroom avoid asking questions for fear of being ridiculed by their colleagues or raising wrong questions. They don't ask questions to avoid being perceived as weak students. In fact, if you ask a question you remain as a fool at that moment. If you don't ask questions and keep doubts within yourself you remain as a fool forever. In addition, if you ask questions, it indicates that you are a good listener and attentive in the classroom. At the same time the educators must also ask questions in the classroom to draw the attention of students and to clarify students' doubts. That is the reason most of the teaching and training programs have question and answer session at the end to clarify the questions as it is not possible to interrupt the teaching and training session. Hence, we will discuss the art of questioning in this chapter.

There are two types of questions—close-ended and open-ended questions. In close-ended question, you expect one word responses while in open-ended question, you expect elaborative responses. Educators can use these two types while teaching as per the situation to ensure effective teaching outcomes.

Questioning and Teaching

> "Good teaching is more a giving of right questions than a giving of right answers."
>
> – *Josef Albers*

I personally adopt questioning as a tool during my teaching and training sessions. To grab the attention of my audience, I shoot questions about the topic in the introduction and in the middle of the session. It keeps the audience alert and stay glued to the session. I shoot both close-ended and open-ended questions. I take feedback from audience by shooting close-ended questions. If I doubt that they don't pay attention through their body language, I shoot open-ended questions so that they will have to get active and respond to my questions. Sometimes I sandwich negative question in my close-ended questions. For instance, I ask once or two as follows: "Have I made it clear to you?" If I am confirmed about their mental presence in the classroom I shoot question as follows: "Have I not made it clear to you?" Embedding this question in the middle of the close-ended questions will help me check the alertness of my audience. If I find that the audience are getting restless and boring, I change my style of teaching immediately by including humor, or varying my pitch to avoid monotony and boredom or including inspiring stories related to the topic. Hence, questioning helps greatly during teaching and training sessions.

Questioning helps the audience not only to be alert but also helps them to think through and relate the theory with practice. It enhances their thinking levels and develops their critical thinking skills. They will be able to imagine more and work rapidly thus broadening their mindset. Therefore, the educators and trainers must use this tool carefully to ensure effective outcomes. To conclude in the words of Chip Bell, "Effective questioning brings insight, which fuels curiosity, which cultivates wisdom."

> "There is no such thing as a worthless conversation, provided you know what to listen for. And questions are the breath of life for a conversation."
>
> – *James Nathan Miller*

***Remember:** Clarify your queries.*

17

Listen Attentively

"We must be silent before we can listen. We must listen before we can learn. We must learn before we can prepare. We must prepare before we can serve. We must serve before we can lead."

– William Arthur Ward

I have a friend of mine—Susan who is older to me in age, and often speaks more and listens less from others. Whenever I try to speak to her I encounter a lot of problems in getting my message across. Whenever I want to speak she won't listen and interrupts and counters with too many questions and often boasts of her achievements. I was happy to listen to her achievements but I was unhappy the way she interfered whenever I wanted to speak.

I advised her to listen to me first and then to speak. Again she goes by her own natural way of interrupting and talking. As a professor in business communication I teach to my eMBA students about effective communication and listening skills. In fact, listening skill is one of the four pillars of business communication, the other three are—speaking, writing, and reading skills. I tried to analyze not only Susan but also a number of people who are poor listeners and have similar listening challenges.

Address Listening Challenges

- We all have an inner dialogue. This is effective throughout the waking hours and it does both good and bad depending on the way we use it. It does good when we know how to convert this inner dialogue positively. We often come across a cliché, "a battle is won twice, first in your mind and then in reality." Whenever you want to achieve your goals you need to create a mental picture of it through visualization, and prepare through your inner dialogue so that you will accomplish your goals as you imagine in your mind first, and do it in reality later. However, when you listen to the speaker this inner dialogue will become inner noise in most of the cases thus disturbing the conversation. It is because this inner noise either anticipates or counters the conversation. And this inner noise becomes more active as one gets older, and we may sometimes find aged people talking within themselves. This is the major culprit of communication. Hence, people should suspend their inner noise to listen attentively and actively.
- Secondly, some listeners have the habit of anticipating what speaker says, and it results in poor listening and interpreting message wrongly. Hence, the listeners must avoid guessing what the speaker says to ensure effective communication.
- Thirdly, some people are egoistic, and they think that they know everything under the sun on the earth. Such egoistic attitude results in ineffective communication. Hence, listeners must shed such attitude, and open their minds with positive attitude to listen and learn from others.
- Fourthly, sometimes there may be external disturbances such as sounds that prevent the listeners from listening effectively. Hence, ensure that there are no abnormal sounds during communication.
- Fifthly, when people are preoccupied with some other tasks, they may not be in a position to listen as they are

concerned about their tasks rather than concentrating on conversation. Hence, ensure that the listener is free from tasks for successful communication.

- Sixthly, when people are depressed with various problems they may not be in a position to absorb what the speaker says. Hence, avoid your past worries, and pay proper attention to the listener to absorb the message.
- Seventhly, when people look at the face of the people more rather than the delivery of the content they may not be able to receive message effectively. Hence, focus on the content, not too much on the face of the speaker.

Research has shown that only 5 per cent of the people are active listeners while the remaining are either average or poor listeners. Being good at listening pays greatly as it shows your respect towards the speaker; minimizes conflicts; and maximizes peace and harmony everywhere. Stephen R. Covey, in his groundbreaking book, *The 7 Habits of Highly Effective People*, reveals that listening is one of the great habits. He states, "Seek first to understand, then to be understood." Hence, listening is one of the greatest habits people often ignore.

Carl Rogers rightly remarked, "Man's inability to communicate is a result of his failure to listen effectively." Hence, listen attentively to ensure effective communication. Remember that listening is a soft skill. When you listen, you respect the other person, and it also shows your keen interest to learn. In addition, if you are a good listener, you learn well and acquire knowledge quickly. If you want to excel as a leader you have to be a good listener. And fortunately listening is a skill that can be acquired through awareness and practice. Hence, address these common listening challenges to develop active listening skills to grow as a successful professional and leader.

> "When people talk, listen completely. Most people never listen."
>
> – *Ernest Hemingway*

***Remember:** Address common listening challenges effectively.*

18

Present Positive Body Language

"The most important thing in communication is hearing what isn't said."

– Peter F. Drucker

Body language plays a crucial role in your communication as it contains 55 percent in communication and the other constituents are: oral language – 7 percent; and voice modulation – 38 percent. You reveal unconscious mind through your body language and conscious mind through your oral language. Therefore, understanding and presenting positive body language improves your chances of success irrespective of the area of interest you are into. For instance, as a student if you present positive body language your educator will be impressed; as an interviewee if you present positive body language your recruiter will be pleased to provide you with an employment opportunity; and as a employee, if you present positive body language at the workplace the people around you will be pleasant leading to your professional success. Hence, there are innumerable advantages associated with presenting positive body language.

Body Language during Interview

Students must demonstrate positive body language during interview. Human Resources (HR) follows the cliché *'hire for attitude and train for skills'*. They look at the attitude of the candidates during interview. They focus more on the body language of the candidates. Hence, the job aspirants must be careful the way they sit and maintain body postures during interview. If they present positive body language they will have better chances of getting the employment offer. Hence, you must understand the right body postures to get an employment offer.

Leaders and their Body Language

Leaders take immense interest to present and project positive body language. Especially during crises leaders present positive body language to avoid panic among their followers to build their confidence. Some leaders like Barack Obama are noted for maintaining poker face before they undertake or oversee major operations and activities. For instance, 72 hours before the Operation Geronimo Obama maintained a poker face despite being aware of the ensuing operation. He performed all functions as usual as though nothing was going to happen. After successfully eliminating Osama he declared his team's achievement. Hence, leaders must know how to maintain their body language neutral in such cases. There are bankers and political leaders who maintain poker faces before declaring major results and achievements to prevent negative fall-out. In fact, there are body language experts who are noted for reading the faces of leaders and celebrities and then advice others about the possible fall-out of their activities. For instance, share market brokers take inputs from body language pundits who observe the body language of the leaders connected with financial market and advice the share market brokers accordingly. Highlighting its importance Bull Deborah rightly remarked, "Body language is a very powerful tool. We had body language before we had speech, and apparently, 80% of what you understand in a conversation is read through the body, not the words." Hence, there is a significant importance attached to body language.

Body Language is Gender and Culture Specific

Study reveals that women are much smarter in understanding the body cues of others. They are smarter in gauging the hidden data of communication such as egos, emotions and feelings. Besides, body language is culture specific because what is considered good in one culture is treated bad in another culture. For instance, some of the Michael Jackson's postures were considered obscene and objectionable in some cultures while they were considered acceptable in other cultures. Hence, you have to be careful with your body language and customize it as per the culture you are into to gain acceptance and establish your credibility.

Body Language is not a Bunch of Hype

Some people criticize body language as a bunch of hype. It is not appropriate as body language is the dominant constituent of any communication. Through body language, intelligence officials can track the culprits. They can identify the liars. When liars speak, their oral language is often inconsistent with their body language because body never lies as it contains 55 percent of communication. And it was substantiated by Martha Graham who rightly said, "The body never lies." Although it is not proved scientifically the lie detector tests go by body language rather than the oral language of the individuals.

Remember the saying, "face is the index of your mind." It is true when we talk of body language. Ancient sages said several things, and of which, body language is a very important one. In this competitive world presenting positive body language gives an edge over others to impress people at the workplace. It creates a positive impression and enhances your professional success. Hence, understand your body language to improve your communication and achieve all-round success.

> "But behavior in the human being is sometimes a defense, a way of concealing motives and thoughts, as language can be a way of hiding your thoughts and preventing communication."
>
> – *Abraham Maslow*

Remember: *Present positive postures.*

19

Be Assertive in the Workplace

"The only healthy communication style is assertive communication"

– Jim Rohn

Arthur works in a research department. One of his colleagues often visits his cubicle, interferes into his work, and wastes his time. She comes to his cubicle, and sits for long time, and talks about her family problems and boasts of her achievements. She would repeat the same stories often and Arthur was distracted from his work, and not in a position to tell her the inconvenience she causes and disturbs his writing work. She is much older to him and he respects her very much because of her age and experience, and of course, her achievements. But he was unable to tell her his predicament for few days. One day when she came to his cubicle Arthur told her, "I was busy with my work and I will talk to you later." She said, "Don't worry! Work will always be there, and it goes on forever!" He said, "If I don't do this work on time my director will scold me." She said, 'don't worry. Take everything easily. Life will go on the way it must go on!" Arthur was not in a position to tell her to quit the place despite being annoyed with her interference and response. He told her firmly not to visit his cubicle often as he was getting busier with his work assignments. She was upset with his response said that he had become head strong, and doesn't have courtesy. From this story, it's obvious that

Arthur was not assertive in the workplace since the beginning. If he were assertive he would have avoided such a predicament. Here are the techniques to follow in the workplace:

Assertive Techniques

Be assertive right from the first day of your employment to convey right signals to other employees. If you're submissive for some time and aggressive for some time you'll encounter workplace challenges in the long run.

When someone approaches you for discussion, indicate the time you want to spend for it so that the visitor fixes within his or her mind the amount of time to be spent with you for discussion. Once the time is over indicate politely that the time is over, and convey clearly that you have to do some other work so that the visitor leaves automatically. If the visitor doesn't get your message, tell firmly but politely that you have some other important tasks to do so that the visitor understands your tasks and leaves the place. Even then the visitor doesn't leave tell repeatedly that you have an important task to do so that the visitor gets your message across and leaves the place. This assertive technique is known as Broken Record Technique where you repeatedly emphasize that time was up and you had to do some other important tasks.

When someone is complaining against you, don't counter it immediately and aggressively. Listen to the person attentively, and analyze the complaint carefully. Don't get offensive or defensive. Explain firmly and politely justifying your stand. Attack the issues, not the individuals. Separate emotions from issues. This assertive technique is known as Fogging.

Whenever any workplace conflict arises, listen to the issues attentively and seek inputs on key aspects through enquiry. It helps you look at the issues objectively, and find out the causes for conflicts to resolve them. Don't accept information either submissively or reject aggressively. This assertive technique is known as Negative Enquiry where you seek inputs through enquiry and clarify assertively.

Whenever workplace tensions rise high, take initiative and listen to all sources so that the tempers cool down. Don't make quick comments or decisions as it adds fuel to the fire. Apply all techniques to cool down the workplace temperature through initiative, listening and empathy. The intention is to listen to all but you must take your call slowly as haste makes waste. Delay your decision-making. This assertive technique is known as Diffusing. Adopt all these four assertive techniques as per the issue, situation through initiative, attentive listening and empathy to ensure workplace peace and harmony. Apart from these assertive techniques observe a few tips as follows:

- Listen to the other person carefully.
- Tell your message clearly instead of attacking others.
- Don't refer 'you'. Instead say, 'I have other tasks to do." It sounds better than pointing your finger at others.
- Use polite and firm language.
- Adopt assertive vocabulary.
- Speak with a smile.
- Maintain positive body language. Make your communication issue-centric, not individual centric.
- Avoid being influenced by others.
- Empathize with others by respecting your rights as well as others' rights.
- Adopt win-win attitude.
- Take feedback from your trusted colleagues about your assertive behavior.
- Above all, practice assertive techniques, and over a period of time you assert yourself and maintain good relations with your colleagues in the workplace.

There are both problems and prospects with assertiveness but it pays to be assertive in the workplace where you can concentrate on your professional tasks without any pressures. It is better than submissiveness where you would suffer silently and would be exploited by others in the workplace. It is also better than aggressiveness where others would suffer with your harsh behavior, and they avoid coming closer to you. Hence, adopt these assertive techniques and tips to be assertive in the workplace to ensure your professional success.

> "The basic difference between being assertive and being aggressive is how our words and behavior affect the rights and well being of others."
>
> – *Sharon Anthony Bower*

Remember: *Practice assertive tools.*

20

Decline Requests Politely

> *"You are not here merely to make a living...You are here to enrich the world, and you impoverish yourself if you forget the errand."*
>
> – Woodrow Wilson

When someone requests you for a favor you find it tough to say 'No' right! When someone phones you for help you find it tough to decline right! Then, you must know how to decline requests assertively without hurting others.

Some of my students and participants from my training programs often request me for favors which I often find it uncomfortable to say 'No' as I hold them with high regards. Sometimes I get invitations for endorsements for their books or to attend meetings and functions, for which I don't get time. I often receive telephone calls seeking succor, and I find myself uncomfortable to say 'No'. One way I'm excited to receive such requests, but at the same time I'm not in a position to accommodate them due to my research and consultancy, and other work pressures. I decided to highlight it in this chapter to help people like me with a few tips overcome from such dilemma.

You must learn how to say 'No' to people's requests. Remember that you cannot please all people as we have only 24 hours in a day, and 365 days in a year. We've our own commitments to our organizations as well as to our family and friends. Hence, you must learn the art of saying 'No' to invitations to create time for yourself, to enjoy, and lead your life happily and successfully. After all, life is short, and we can't afford to concentrate on superfluous activities. At the same time, it's also advisable to please people as much as you can as they have expectations from you. Being a celebrity is not a cakewalk especially when you want to serve others like a servant leader. Hence, you must acquire the art of saying 'No' firmly but politely. Here are the tools and techniques to decline assertively to invitations:

- Communicate that you are busy at the moment so that you can attend the request in future depending on the availability of time.
- Suggest an alternative outlet where the sender can get the things done, if possible.
- Inform that presently you're overscheduled with engagements and you'll get back to the sender when you find time.
- Don't undermine or insult the sender.
- Be tactful and polite. Empathize with the sender.
- Present your decline politely but firmly.
- Refuse positively and end with goodwill.

Adopt Fourth A

To decline a request people usually adopt three styles such as attacking, avoiding, and accommodating. Here is the fourth style of asserting yourself wherein both the sender and you are happy with the outcome as the former is happy with assertive response and you are happy as you find time to engage in your other productive activities. Convey firmly but politely, and we call it assertively to ensure that there is no ill-will, and you can leave with a good impression. Thomas Sowell rightly remarked, "Politeness and consideration for others is like investing pennies and getting dollars back."

Sample Templates

1. Here is the response of attacking, "Thank you for the invitation, but I am afraid that I have to decline."
2. Here is the response of avoiding, "Thank you for your invitation. I currently have other commitments. If anything changes in my schedule, I will certainly let you know."
3. Here is the response of accommodating, "Thanks for your request, and I'll do the needful."
4. Here is the response of asserting, "Thank you for that opportunity, but my humility must keep me in check."

Sandwich Decline

Adopt 'yes-no-yes' formula like sandwich feedback where we correct the negative behavior of the person while giving feedback starting with a praise, concluding with a praise and correcting the negative behavior in the middle. Similarly, start with a congratulatory note followed by your inability to favor citing the reasons succinctly, and conclude with wishes. William Ury, a Harvard professor authored a brilliant book titled, *The Power of a Positive No: How to Say No and Still Get to Yes* highlighting this method of polite decline to invitations. Here are the sample templates for your reference to decline assertively:

Template #1: Rejection of a Book Proposal by a Publisher

Dear Marshall,

We are glad to receive your book proposal, and we read it thoroughly. It is very interesting covering various aspects of leadership lessons. However, we will not be able to pursue it for publication. Current policy is to publish books for the academic market only, and with a minimum word count of approximately 80,000. For these reasons we are afraid this book is not suitable for us.

We wish you the best of luck with your proposal, and thank you again for allowing us the time to give it full consideration.

Best regards,

Steve

Template #2 - Declining a Request for Book Endorsement

Dear Mark,

Thank you for your e-mail requesting an endorsement for your new book.

I have put a moratorium on offering endorsements. My travel schedule and business commitments prevent me from giving your book the attention it deserves in order to provide an appropriate endorsement.

I wish you well in your publishing endeavor.

David

Template #3 - Declining a Request for Book Endorsement

Dear Alex,

Congratulations on the new book!

Thank you for your kind invitation to write an endorsement for your book. I greatly appreciate you thinking of me. As much as I would like to publicly commend your work, I currently have other commitments that would inhibit my ability to do your book justice.

If anything changes in my schedule, I will certainly let you know.

Warm Regards

Myka

When someone approaches you for a favor you are in his/her good books, and on his/her mind. It means the person holds you with great respect. Hence, treat the sender politely, by telling your time constraints. Most of the achievers have a heart to help others because they know the pain to touch the tipping point but they don't find time to accommodate invitations. However, they can appoint employees who are good at etiquette, and who maintain confidentiality to handle such favors.

Learn to say 'No' assertively and respectfully without hurting others. If you take too much workload you lose track of your time line, and you end up nowhere. Your deadlines and commitments are important, and at the same time ensure that the sender is pleased with your response. You need to strike a balance between your personal and professional commitments, and your social obligations. It is easier said than done.

Remember not to be rude with your requests. Saying 'No' requires etiquette. It requires great tact and diplomacy especially when your know people, and more so to your fans and followers who admire you for your outstanding achievements and contributions. In addition, when you are approached with an invitation the sender has regards to you, and expectations from you. Hence, make sure that the sender understands your constraints; empathizes with you; and feels happy with your polite response. It is tough to climb the tree but it is easy to have a free fall from the top. Similarly, it is tough to climb the ladder of success and easy to fall from the top. When you achieve success in a hard way you must learn to sustain it. And, your humility index must go up along with your success. Hence, be humble and decline assertively to have an everlasting impression on the senders.

> "I shall pass this way but once. Therefore any good that I can do, or any kindness that I can show, let me do it now for I shall not pass this way again."
>
> – *William Penn*

Remember: *Observe etiquette.*

21

Avoid Massaging Your Boss's Ego

> *"People ask the difference between a leader and a boss.... The leader works in the open, and the boss in covert. The leader leads and the boss drives."*
>
> – Theodore Roosevelt

The caption of this chapter probably puts you in a fix whether you have to massage your boss's ego. Before we arrive at a conclusion there are various aspects to know such as the difference between a boss and a leader, and four models from organizational behavior (OB).

OB Models

There are four models in organizational behavior namely autocratic, custodial, supportive and collegial. The autocratic model prevailed initially where employees were under the mercy of employers. In this model, the employees worked as labor and obeyed whatever the bosses ordered. Subsequently surfaced another model named custodial where the employees cannot be fired as they are provided with job security and other financial and non-financial benefits. It is further followed by another model named supportive where employees are supported by employers and bosses above them. It is fairly better than the previous models of autocratic and custodial. Currently we have collegial model where there is no much gap between the superiors and subordinates as all are treated with request equally. The

Generation Y appreciates this collegial model, and it is mostly followed by American management and top global companies in the world. In this model, there will not be any bosses but only leaders. However, we still find bosses in the guise of leaders.

Bosses versus Leaders

In fact, there is a difference between bosses and leaders as bosses are mostly arrogant and egoistic in nature and they often come with workaholic attitude. Russell H. Ewing differentiates between bosses and leaders as follows: "A boss creates fear, a leader confidence. A boss fixes blame, a leader corrects mistakes. A boss knows all, a leader asks questions. A boss makes work drudgery, a leader makes it interesting." The people who work with bosses find it tough to get along with them as the expectations of the bosses are high and they are mostly task oriented. In contrast, the leaders are blend of both task-orientation and people-orientation with a heart to make a difference in the lives of their employees. The leaders adopt transformational leadership style, and treat their subordinates like colleagues and get the tasks executed successfully. The leaders support the subordinates in their training and development and quicken their career advancement. They empathize and listen to their subordinates and lead their teams successfully.

If you happen to work under a boss you have to be more careful in your work. As long as you do your work sincerely you don't have to bother about your boss, and you don't have to massage his or her ego. All that you must do is to be assertive in your approach, actions and communication.

Tips to Handle Your Boss

- Handle your boss with tactness but not at the cost of your integrity and principles. Be in his or her good books to get the tasks executed smoothly. At the same time, learn to draw the line between praise and flattery.
- Be strong in your domain so that you will have respect in the workplace and boss will not have any scope to point you out.

- Avoid arguing with your boss because there is a popular cliché — *'boss is always right'*. Therefore, keep your views within yourself. When the organizational issues are involved express your views assertively.
- Be professional and avoid interfering into his or her personal life to maintain longevity in relations.
- Don't surprise your boss. Keep your boss informed whenever you do important tasks. The boss should not feel that s/he was bypassed or neglected.
- Emphasize on ideas rather than individuals in organizational aspects to avoid getting into egoistic issues.
- Keep your boss in good humor to avoid organizational politics and ensure peaceful workplace ambience.

It is often said in the corporate world that people don't leave organizations but they leave bad bosses. It is mostly correct as organizations are often good but the people who lead often found to be problematic for the employees. Therefore, instead of blaming the bad bosses, it is better to understand your boss well and mould yourself accordingly to build a chemistry and compatibility to get the things going smoothly. You cannot choose your bosses and just because of bad bosses you cannot shift organizations frequently. Hence, best thing is to understand the ground realities and personality types; and build a chemistry to enable peaceful workplace ambience and outcome.

> "In the past a leader was a boss. Today's leaders must be partners with their people... they no longer can lead solely based on positional power."
>
> – *Ken Blanchard*

Remember: *Build compatibility with your boss.*

22

Make Your Decision Wisely

> *"Anyone who thinks that intuition is a substitute for reason is indulging in a risky delusion. Detached from rigorous analysis, intuition is a fickle and undependable guide-it is as likely to lead to disaster as to success."*
>
> – Eric Bonabeau

Making decisions is easier said than done. Some people think that all decisions they make must be successful. Most of the people think that their decisions go wrong most of the times. In fact, how others think about the impact of their decisions nobody knows as nobody reveals what is there in their minds and declares their failures in decision-making. The truth is that most of the decisions go wrong for most of the people as decision-making depends on various factors such as head, heart, gut and the prevailing situation around them.

Decision making is a Herculean task as the outcomes are unpredictable because we make decisions based on our head, heart, gut; and either based on our past experiences or from others' experience. In love matter, people often go by their heart, not by head or gut. In the organizational issues, people often go by their head and gut. And in some special instances, people go by their head, heart and gut to make their decisions. Of course, there is no quick-fix approach to decision-making. The people who encounter failures frequently keep their reserves ready and keep different plans such as Plan A, Plan B, and Plan C, etc.

I was asked to lead a webinar by International Leadership Association on "Soft Leadership" on August 29, 2012 which is a new leadership perspective I have coined. I prepared thoroughly on the topic, rehearsed many time by improving the draft and including new ideas and insights in every subsequent draft. I also engaged my two sons to ensure the success of the webinar. Unfortunately at the last moment, there was a problem with my internet connection and I along with my son rushed to a nearby browsing centre and led the webinar successfully. We booked the place at the browsing centre in advance as a standby, and it saved us from the predicament. Before moving out to lead the webinar, I asked my younger son about the internet connection whether it would work out. He said that he would fix the problem. But I had an apprehension that fixing the problem at the time just before the webinar would delay the session. Hence, I followed my intuition and quickly moved outside and led the webinar at the internet browsing center which was close to my residence.

Hence, whenever you make a decision, don't assume that everything will go smoothly. Be prepared from distractions and external challenges. Be mentally prepared that all decisions may not turn out to be fruitful. Whenever the outcomes are negative, learn lessons and move forward as such unpleasant experiences and outcomes will enhance your intuition thus improving your decision-making skills.

There are various ways you can make decisions. When you have full information you can make decision based on your head. When you have partial information, you can go by your head and heart. If you don't have any information, you can go by your gut. Leaders at the top level often work under uncertainty and complexity. When they don't have access to appropriate information they go by their intuition.

Benjamin Franklin's Decision Making

Benjamin adopted the following methodology to ensure successful outcome from his decisions:

My way is to divide half a sheet of paper by a line into two columns, writing over the one Pro, and over the other Con. Then during three or four days' consideration I put down under the different heads short hints of the different motives that at different times occur to me for or against the measure. When I have thus got them all together in one view, I endeavor to estimate their respective weights, and where I find two, one on each side, that seem equal, I strike them both out. If I find a reason pro equal to some two reasons con, I strike out the three. If I judge some two reasons con equal to some three reasons pro, I strike out the five; and thus proceeding I find at length where the balance lies.

My Method of Decision-Making

William Pollard once remarked, "It is not always what we know or analyzed before we make a decision that makes it a great decision. It is what we do after we make the decision to implement and execute it that makes it a good decision."

I often make decisions as follows: If I am sure about the outcome, I go by gut feelings. If I am not an expert on the issue, I consult various experts and take their viewpoints. I weigh the pros and cons by using both my head and heart. If pros outnumber the cons then I make the decision. I don't regret once I make a decision because I make decisions based on the prevailing circumstances and constraints. However, if the outcomes are negative, I would learn lessons from them and ensure that I don't make such mistakes in future. I treat every failure as a learning experience and move forward with energy and enthusiasm following the sage advice: "Good decisions come from experience, and experience comes from bad decisions."

Albert Camus remarked, "Life is the sum of all your choices." Hence, don't waste your precious time by brooding over your wrong decisions. Instead, learn lessons and invest the present time for making successful decisions in future. To conclude, you make decisions based on your head. You make commitment based on your heart. You execute tasks based on your gut. Hence, blend your head, heart and gut proportionately and act as per the situation to achieve the desired outcomes in your life.

> "The hardest thing to learn in life is which bridge to cross and which to burn."
>
> – *David Russell*

Remember: *Decision determines your destiny.*

REFERENCE

Decision Making - Harvard Business Review Series

23

Be Resourceful

"If you think you are beaten, you are. If you think you dare not, you don't! If you want to win, but think you can't, it's almost a cinch you won't. If you think you'll lose, you're lost; for out in the world we find. Success begins with a fellow's will; it's all in the state of the mind. Life's battles don't always go to the stronger and faster man, but sooner or later the man who wins is the man who thinks he can."

– Walter D. Wintle

If you want to achieve success in life you must accept responsibility when the situation demands and work with what you have rather than blaming for not being equipped with all resources. However, some people have the habit of inventing excuses for their failures and making others as scapegoats. To be successful in your life, you must be resourceful. We will discuss the importance of being resourceful in this chapter.

Research shows that people waste 30 percent of their time thinking about their past that cannot be changed. Instead of being bogged down about their past, the resourceful people concentrate on the present to make future for themselves. While concentrating on the present they manage both the internal and external distractions which are mostly responsible either for delayed execution or failures. If they find that they could not achieve due to internal distractions, they analyze the reasons; take quick actions; discipline themselves; and move forward.

If they find that the external distractions are a cause to worry they try to manage their best to get things back on their track. If they find that external distractions are due to the influence of external environment, they don't waste their time in brooding over them. In contrast, they concentrate on other activities on which they have control. Hence, resourceful people are smart, and their main intention is to execute the tasks by any means within the available resources. In armed forces, soldiers should not waste food. In addition, a soldier must learn to work with what he has. He cannot blame his tools. He has to find out the techniques to get the tasks executed effectively with the tools he has to win the war.

The resourceful people emphasize on ideas rather than on blaming individuals and brooding too much on issues. It is rightly said that below average people talk about individuals, average people talk about individuals and above average individuals talk about ideas. Therefore, the resourceful people look at the issues seriously and explore various options to address them and find the solutions accordingly. When you look at soldiers they are resourceful as they have to work under tons of trials and tribulations and constraints. They undergo training to develop the mindset to be resourceful. At the time of recruitment, the interview members ask several questions to check for spontaneity and resourcefulness. Only the aspirants who have these two will have the competitive edge over others to get recruited into armed forces.

Remember to be resourceful during recession. Tough times call for tough decisions. People must learn to work with what they have rather than blaming others and external distractions. Distractions are part of life. The more the distractions the higher must be your will-power. If you are resourceful you will be able to save your time, money and energy. Your effectiveness enhances and dependence on others decreases. You will build more confidence in yourself. You develop the habit of working within your limitations and people around you appreciate your abilities and capabilities.

Work with What You Have

Work with the money you have; the knowledge you have; and the manpower you have. Remember that it is the bad tradesman who blames his tools. Don't blame others. Learn to look at opportunities rather than threats. Don't blame parents, friends, and relatives. Don't make others as a scapegoat. Take responsibility and work with what you have. Show to the world that you worked despite limitations. Don't create hype but live with hope that one day you will be on the top of the world where the entire world looking at your achievements questioning, "How did small man achieve big silently?"

Develop Resourceful-Mindset

> "When you are inspired by some great purpose, some extraordinary project, all your thoughts break their bounds. Your mind transcends limitations, your consciousness expands in every direction and you find yourself in a new, great and wonderful world. Dormant forces, faculties and talents become alive, and you discover yourself to be a greater person by far than you ever dreamed yourself to be."
>
> – *Patanjali*

I often work within my own resources. I don't have any website but I have created three blogs, one Speaker Mix and Facebook page, and post my ideas on them and share my knowledge. I don't have a separate computer system. My two sons and I share one computer system. I don't have any regular income but I manage through the income earned from my training programs. I don't blame others and God for putting me under pressure as I often look at opportunities out of threats to lead from the front. I often think about the door that is opened rather than the one that is closed. I cannot afford to buy books but I manage going to libraries and read. I also visit prestigious blogs and acquire knowledge. Hence, I succeeded as I never blamed others but worked with what I had. If you work in this way, you can achieve success much easily. Hence, develop the mindset to be resourceful and work with what you have to achieve success quickly.

Conclusion

Most of the achievers are resourceful at heart. They worked with what they had. They did not blame their tools and improved their techniques to execute their tasks effectively. They didn't blame circumstances. They converted their threats into opportunities and succeeded. Whether you want to be a Mark Zuckerberg, Michael Jordan or Malcom Gladwell, you must learn to be resourceful to leave a mark behind. Hence, be resourceful to make it big in your life.

> "People are always blaming their circumstances for what they are. I don't believe in circumstances. The people who get on in this world are the people who get up and look for the circumstances they want, and, if they can't find them, make them."
>
> – *George Bernard Shaw*

Remember: *Work with what you have.*

24

Maintain Work-Life Balance

"Life is indeed beautiful. It's times when we sink into our hectic and stressful lifestyles that we are blinded and fail to see what we really have."

– Unknown

Work-life balance has gained importance due to the complexity and uncertainty involved in the present world both at workplace and home. There are instances where people make tons of money but cannot find time to enjoy their lives; and there are people who don't get money at all to survive in this world. It is a contradiction but a reality in the world. Hence, organizations are giving significant importance to extend facilities to their employees to relax at the workplace so that employees find time for their personal life apart from enhancing organizational productivity.

What is Work-Life Balance?

Work–life balance is a concept based on balancing your personal, professional and social life to provide meaning to your life. It should not be confused as a tight-rope walk between workplace commitments and domestic demands. It is about understanding your priorities in your personal, professional and social life and acting in a balanced way. It is also about taking a time off from your work schedules to pursue your hobbies and unwind yourself.

Workholism

> "I arise in the morning torn between the desire to improve the world and a desire to enjoy the world. This makes it hard to plan the day."
>
> – *E.B.White*

Workholism is all about doing lots of work at the cost of personal and social life. It leads to health hazards. According to Barbara Killinger, "Workaholism is a soul destroying addiction that changes people's personalities and the values they live by. A workaholic is a work-obsessed individual who had gradually become emotionally crippled and addicted to power and control." And Spence and Robbins defined workaholic as follows: "Workaholic is a person who exhibits three properties: high work involvement, feeling driven to work because of inner pressures, low in enjoyment of work." Hence, people must draw the line between hard work and workhalism. They must remember that all the work no play makes the Jack dull.

The employees must be able to strike the right balance between work and life. There is a strong need to take time off from their routine work. They should plan for vacations or tours to relieve their stress. At the workplace too, the employees should take regular breaks after lunch, do light physical exercises and talk to their colleagues. At home, it is necessary to do yoga or mediation or physical exercises to ease their stress levels so that they can go for work with renewed energy and enthusiasm.

Tips to Maintain Work-Life Balance

> "If you are losing your leisure, look out; you may be losing your soul"
>
> – *Logan P. Smith*

- Pursue your passionate areas as you don't feel that you are working anymore because you enjoy doing your work with involvement.
- Avoid the psychological apprehension that if you don't work you will fail and fall behind.

- Set some realistic boundaries and stick to them religiously.
- Be assertive and don't say 'yes' to unreasonable requests at the workplace.
- Delegate your tasks that don't invite your attention.
- Don't mix up your personal life with professional life. Demarcate them to avoid spill over. Theodore Roosevelt rightly remarked, "When you play, play hard; when you work, don't play at all."
- Spend some time to reflect and refuel yourself.
- Stay away from multitasking. Do one task at a time to enhance effectiveness.
- Avail 'flexi time' facility as some companies provide such options to enable you to work as per your convenience and work from home as well thus saving your time spent through commuting.
- Spend some time in solitude.
- Hit gym regularly and maintain sound health.
- Don't spend too much time on internet and cell phones. Don't watch television for long hours.
- Forget unpleasant moments in your life. Focus on present and move forward with optimism.
- Promise less and deliver more.
- Remember that money is not everything. It is needed only for your survival.
- Above all, have the attitude of gratitude.

Follow 8:8:8 Principle

We are gifted with 24 hours in a day. We must spend 8 hours of our time for work; 8 hours for sleep; 8 hours for other activities. It provides meaning for your life and you don't have to regret at your death-bed for not enjoying your life meaningfully. Remember that you must enjoy the journey of your life to reach your destination of success.

Organizational Initiatives

Most of the companies have 5 day week to enable the employees work hard and take a break for 2 days to party hard and enjoy their lives. They also provide paid holidays to enable their employees to travel and unwind. At the workplace also, some companies provide meditation, yoga and other facilities like recreation to enable the employees to balance work and life. Therefore, employees must make use of such facilities and spend their time to unwind and relax themselves. In fact, such measures enhance productivity and performance thus achieving organizational excellence and effectiveness.

Presently people find several materialistic comforts due to the rapid growth in technology but they don't enjoy the life the way they want due to work pressures, deadlines and competition. In addition, the aspirations and expectations of the people are growing tremendously. It compels companies constantly to be on the lookout for innovative products and features to meet the rising expectations of the people. It boils down to more expectations from employees resulting in more pressure on employees. Hence, employees must understand the current scenario and take precautions about their health and balance their work and life.

It is a myth to say that you have either work or life. The truth is that life is meaningful if there is work, and work is meaningful if you enjoy your life. To conclude, it is time we draw the line between competition and collaboration; and work and life to lead life happily and successfully.

> "No matter how busy you are, or how busy you think you are, the work will always be there tomorrow, but your friends might not be."
>
> – *Unknown*

Remember: *Balance your personal, professional and social life.*

25

Broaden Your Circle of Friends

"Success is a cooperative effort; it's dependent upon those who stand beside you."

– Jon M. Huntsman Sr.

Aristotle said, "Man is a social animal. He cannot live alone." It is true as having association with others is a social need not only for animals but also for human beings. As man needs food, cloth, shelter and sex he also desires to associate with others to share his emotions, feelings, and interests. Therefore, he makes friends. We will discuss broadening circle of friends and network that help you broaden your prospects in all spheres. When you broaden your circle of friends, personally you get a lot of satisfaction to share your thoughts; professionally you can exchange ideas and grow; and socially you can create impact on others and build your image and brand.

When you network you connect with many people in your area of interest and enhance your visibility. People within your circle will recognize that you have a specific set of skills, knowledge, and abilities. They can refer you to others for professional assignments. They can also refer you to NGOs (Non-Government Organizations) where you can share your knowledge without any monetary gains thus elevating your stature. In the present world, who you know is more important that what you know. There are many people who have a huge potential but they don't have the right connections to display and excel. In fact, a right person at the right place and right time will make him or her stand out from others.

Tips to Broaden Your Circle of Friends

> "It's all about people. It's about networking and being nice to people and not burning any bridges."
>
> – *Mike Davidson*

- Remember the names of the people and their important events. Find out their areas of interest and create a common ground to connect with them.
- Be gracious in praising others. But understand the difference between praise and flattery. When you are specific in praise people will take your praise seriously and connect with you quickly.
- Pursue your hobbies. You can meet many people and broaden your circle.
- Develop charisma and improve your communication skills to connect with others.
- Maintain a unique professional dress code to stand out from others.
- Take membership in professional associations and bodies in your area of interest.
- Contribute articles in trade journals and magazines to enhance your visibility. Lead webinars as a thought leader. It invites attention and more people join in your network.
- Take initiative to deliver speeches and provide presentations.
- Never think of '*what is in it for me.*' Think of what value you would add to others and the difference you make in the lives of others.
- Never expect anything from others because the other person might not be in a position to reciprocate when you extended your hand. The person may have his or her own constraints. Remember that what goes around comes around in a different form.

How to Network in Social Gatherings?

> "More business decisions occur over lunch and dinner than at any other time, yet no MBA courses are given on the subject."
>
> – *Peter Drucker*

- When you go for a meeting or public event reach well ahead of time so that you can find likeminded people and chat with them. It becomes easier for you to connect with others easily.
- Observe the people around you closely and take initiative to introduce yourself and start conversation with proper eye contact.
- Ask few questions and listen to them attentively. Praise them sincerely. Avoid tooting your horn as people don't appreciate it.
- Keep your business cards ready and give when asked. Also take others' cards with etiquette for your future reference.

Currently we have various online social and professional networking sites such as Facebook, LinkedIn and Twitter, etc. Make use of them to broaden your network of friends.

Diane Darling outlines in her book, *Networking for Career Success: 24 Lessons for Getting to Know the Right People* as follows: "networking is the art of building and sustaining mutually beneficial relationships. In other words, one should expect to give as well as receive." Hence, networking is a two-way street with give and take and make sure that you approach others with a positive mindset to build lasting relations. Broadening circle of friends is easier said than done as it takes time, energy and resources. Once you broaden your circle you must know how to maintain it. Remember that broadening your circle of friends is a way of life. It should not be done only when you need them. On the other hand, it should be done a continuous process to excel as a successful professional and leader.

"The successful networkers I know, the ones receiving tons of referrals and feeling truly happy about themselves, continually put the other person's needs ahead of their own."

– Bob Burg

Remember: *Build mannerism and charisma.*

26

Build Your Leadership Brand

"Just as a product or service brand creates value over generic products or services for its owners, we believe that a corporate brand is sustained and enhanced by that organization's leadership brand. Leadership brand represents the identity and reputation of leaders throughout a company. Leaders demonstrate a brand when they think and act in ways congruent with the desired product or firm brand."

– Dave Ulrich

When you look at corporate leaders such as Richard Branson of Virgin, Steve Jobs of Apple and Scott Monty of Ford there is one common thread connecting all of them – they have all successfully built their leadership brands. We will discuss leadership branding in this chapter.

What is Leadership Branding?

As we brand products the leaders must brand themselves. Leadership branding is all about branding yourself to get noticed for good reasons rather than wrong reasons. Leadership is a brand. It is more than an aspiration and comes with inspiration. Leadership comes when you lead in your passionate area. If you are the best in your passionate area then you are the leader. Hence, leadership branding can be defined as the process of building your leadership brand consistently in your domain as per your vision to get distinguished and stand out from others. People can easily recall you when you brand yourself in a specific area. Renowned management thinkers, Dave Ulrich and Norm Smallwood are specialists in leadership branding and leadership code. They have written a book on leadership branding, *Leadership Brand: Developing Customer-Focused Leaders to Drive Performance and Build Lasting Value* and published articles in this area. According to Norm Smallwood leadership brand is outwardly focused and is based on other's expectations.

Advantages

> "Even individuals need to develop a brand for themselves .... Whatever your area of expertise, you can take steps to make people think of YOU when they think of your field."
>
> – *Accelepoint Webzine*

There are several merits involved in building your leadership brand. Personally, it strengthens your CV and enhances your market value. You will have great demand and you don't have to worry about losing your job as you will have a number of employment offers thrown open. Professionally, it builds confidence among the stakeholders such as employees, customers, suppliers, shareholders, governmental organization and other affiliated bodies.

Leaders must build their brands but they should believe more in doing work rather than being conscious about their brands to achieve the desired outcomes. Failure to do so leads to damaging their brand image and losing their goodwill. Leadership brand must be created keeping the customers' and clients' aspirations and expectations in view to build the brand quickly and ensure its longevity.

Leadership Branding for Students

Students must learn how to brand themselves to succeed professionally. Leaders like Richard Branson, Steve Jobs and Marshall Goldsmith to name a few are all successful because they realized their inherent strengths; worked passionately throughout their lives; and learned continuously to stand out from others. Similarly, you must understand the importance of branding in the educational institution itself to get recognized and build your brand successfully. Hence, realize its importance in the early age itself and carve a niche for yourself to get noticed. There are professional sites like LinkedIn where you can build your brand consistently. You can also create blog and start posting your ideas and insights in your area of interest so that you find visitors in your area following it and building a network around yourself over a period of time. You can register online websites of your area of interest and you can join associations to network and build a circle around yourself. Deliver speeches and presentations in your area of interest. Contribute articles in trade journals and other prestigious journals as that help you get noticed quickly. Above all, don't dilute your brand once you have carved a niche for yourself to avoid starting from the scratch again.

Brand Building Tips

Everyone craves for building their brand. But very few people are aware of the tools and techniques essential to build their brands. Here are the tips to build your leadership brand:

- When you want to build a brand for yourself, be clear with what you want to achieve. Look at your strengths and craft a vision statement and then build your brand consistently and constantly.
- Follow the road less travelled. For instance, Steve Jobs followed the road less travelled and excelled as an innovative guru.
- Focus on your core strengths.
- You can quickly build your brand when you can give what others want rather than giving what you have. Remember to realign your strengths as per the expectations and aspirations of the people around you to build your brand successfully.
- Stay relevant by reinventing yourself as per the changing external environment.

- Work in your passionate area for 10,000 hours continuously to acquire competencies and capabilities to build your professional image.
- Excel as a knowledge leader and thought leader as it helps enhance your credibility and build unique leadership brand.
- You can use your e-mail signature to brand yourself the way you want. Whenever you send e-mails the receiver might read them and click the links and get to know about you and remember you.
- You can upload your profile in LinkedIn, Twitter, Facebook, Google + and your blogs to build your brand. You can also have your website with the activities that you do and offer to others.
- Send newsletter either weekly or monthly in your area of interest to the subscribers who enjoy reading and might approach you with consulting offers or training programs.
- Lead webinars, provide guest lectures, and conduct workshops to reach out to the people.
- Join NGOs (Non-Governmental Organizations) and share your knowledge freely. For instance, Peter Drucker contributed greatly through NGOs and it helped him brand as a management thinker and legend globally.
- Ask testimonials from your clients and post them in your website. You can share the online links with others and gain their confidence quickly.
- Above all, make a difference in the lives of others.

3-Step Process to Build Your Leadership Brand

"Branding demands commitment; commitment to continual re-invention; striking chords with people to stir their emotions; and commitment to imagination. It is easy to be cynical about such things, much harder to be successful."

– Sir Richard Branson, CEO of Virgin

Adopt the following three-step process to build your brand:

1. Excel as an expert. To become an expert, focus on your passionate area. Find out your innate talents rather than focusing on skills. Talents are inborn which people acquire from their parents. People have talents by birth. They must spot their talents and tap them. Then they have to focus clearly on their goals and build skills around their inborn talents. In this way, they can grow as experts.
2. Share your knowledge with others. You cannot reach out to entire audience physically. Hence, you must author books in your area of interest so that you can reach out to the world. You can also blog articles in your area.
3. Interact with people in your core area. When you interact with people they will pose questions about your domain knowledge. You can do research in those areas and improve your knowledge base constantly. This physical interaction builds connections with others thus enhancing your visibility and promoting your leadership brand.

Succinctly, focus on your talents and build skills around it; share your knowledge through your books; and interact with likeminded people to grow in your area of interest to build your leadership brand. Remember that your leadership brand value is your identity and the reflection of your credibility. Create and build your leadership brand through right tools and techniques and ensure that you sustain throughout your life to live like a legend and leave a lasting legacy for others.

> "What I know for sure is that if you want to have success, you can't make success your goal. The key is not to worry about being successful, but to instead work toward being significant – and the success will naturally follow."
>
> – *Oprah Winfrey*

***Remember:** Enhance your market value.*

27

Love Your Mother, But Don't Hate Another Person's Mother

"Anger and intolerance are the enemies of correct understanding."

– Mahatma Gandhi

Presently people across the globe are getting impatient, intolerant, and agitated without any concern for others. It seems there is less respect towards others' religions, regions, races, languages, ethnicities, cultures, and communities. In addition, the aspirations and expectations from all stakeholders are rising rapidly. For instance, children demand more from parents; students demand more from teachers; subordinates demand more from superiors; employees demand more from employers; followers demand more from leaders; and people demand more from the government. In fact, people are becoming more rights-oriented rather than duty-oriented. They must remember John F. Kennedy's clarion call: "Ask not what your country can do for you; ask what you can do for your country."

There must be a shift in the mindset of the people. There must be a need for tolerance and respect towards others. People must be duty-oriented rather than rights-oriented. Empathy is the answer for these challenges. Empathy is the ability to step into the shoes of others, and look at the issues from others' perspective. However, presently people hardly empathize with others. When we empathize with others most of the global challenges and conflicts will be resolved easily. Through empathy, we can put an end to intolerance, impatience, and instability. Through empathy, we can resolve several global challenges amicably. In fact, empathy is essential for global peace, prosperity, and stability.

Some people resort to violence to settle their scores. And some countries wage wars to settle their long-pending issues. In fact, violence is not the solution to several global issues. Ralph Waldo Emerson rightly remarked, "Peace cannot be achieved through violence, it can only be attained through understanding." People should shed their violent attitude and must respect others through empathy and understanding.

It is essential to respect all religions, regions and communities in the world. To be born in a community is not our choice, but a chance. Therefore, understand others, respect their beliefs, cultures and views with empathy to gain acceptance from everyone and to leave a good impression.

Love your mother but don't hate another person's mother. As your mother is precious to you, another person's mother is equally precious to him. As your race, religion, region, language, ethnicity, culture, and community are precious to you, they are equally precious to others.

William J. Clinton said, "The real differences around the world today are not between Jews and Arabs; Protestants and Catholics; Muslims, Croats, and Serbs. The real differences are between those who embrace peace and those who would destroy it; between those who look to the future and those who cling to the past; between those who open their arms and those who are determined to clench their fists." People must learn to empathize with others to make a difference in the lives of others. We need empathetic leaders like Mahatma Gandhi, Martin Luther King Jr, Mother Teresa, Desmond Tutu and Dalai Lama to name a few to maintain global peace, security and stability. Remember what Mother Teresa said when asked what you can do to promote world peace: "Go home and love your family." As charity begins at home, let us start promoting global peace by loving our family and empathizing with others first.

"The test of courage comes when we are in the minority.
The test of tolerance comes when we are in the majority."

– *Ralph W. Sockman*

***Remember:** Respect all communities.*

28

Be Proud of Being an Indian

> *"If there is one place on the face of earth where all the dreams of living men have found a home from the very earliest days when man began the dream of existence, it is India."*
>
> – Romain Rolland, French Nobel Laureate

Many centuries ago India was the leader across the world. We have the oldest civilization in the world. We taught the world about religions. We taught the world about tolerance. We taught the world about universal brotherhood. We taught the world the meaning of life. We taught the world about Vedas, and we shared the greatest knowledge on the earth. We had one of the oldest universities in the earth – Nalanda. We were strong in several spheres. Ashoka was a global leader and excelled as an emperor who put India on the world map through his visionary leadership. But we lost everything to the West. Why did we lose it? It is due to lack of unity among us, and lack of visionary leaders among us.

Individuals often take intrapersonal feedback to improve upon themselves. Similarly, Indians have to take feedback about India and Indians so that they can improve themselves. Here is the feedback about India and Indians:

We Indians waste a lot of time in resolving issues arising out of incompetence. We have stopped taking charge of situations. If there is an accident on the road, people will stop and watch.

They will all wait for government officials to come forward and tell everybody what to do. What kind of a people are we? What kind of attitude do we Indians have? We need to have a shift in mindset, and change in attitude to make India a great country in the world.

We Indians are great in Mathematics and Information Technology. We have the third largest technical manpower on the earth. We have the second largest population in the world which is a great asset for Indians. For the first time in history we have 400 million young people who are the backbone of India and who can make India a prosperous country and become a super power in the world.

Strengths: We are tolerant and patriotic. We believe in fraternity and universal brotherhood. We are emotional, and forgive others quickly and forget our negative past. We are flexible, receptive, and accommodative. We are blessed with rich natural resources. We have the high savings rate, and strong family values and system. We believe in unity in diverisity. We are the largest democracy, and the fastest growing economy in the world.

Weaknesses: We don‘t have great leaders who can set a strong vision and inspire others. We are not punctual, and we talk too much. Corruption has become a cancer to Indian society. We don‘t have strong infrastructure. We have sevearal challenges such as illiteracy, child labour, and dowry to name a few. We have a press which believes in sensanalisation rather than highlighting developmental activities for building a strong nation. We have an education system that encourages memory rather than allow us to think critically, analyse logically, and apply effectively. Above all, we have the employability problem rather than unemployement problem.

There are many Indian leaders who glorified India and sacrificed their lives for the cause of India. However, it is Swami Vivekananda and Mahatma Gandhi who are the pride of India as they have changed the face of India globally. Swami Vivekananda showed to the world that India is the mother of all religions in the world. The Indian land sheltered many religions and communities with a universal brotherhood. This land of India taught the world about non-violence and peace. This land of India taught the world that freedom can be acquired through peaceful means under the soft leadership of Mahatma Gandhi. This land taught the world that all religions can live together peacefully under one roof with unity in diversity.

Why Mahatma Gandhi was never awarded the Nobel Peace Prize? He was considered above the Nobel Prize. There were 5 top leaders in the world who were followers of Mahatma Gandhi and received the Nobel Prize - Martin Luther King Jr, Nelson Mandela, Dalai Lama, Aung San Sui Kyi, and Barack Obama. In fact, there is no international prize that can measure the greatness of Mahatma Gandhi. Mohandas Karamchand Gandhi was above everything. That is why he was called Mahatma (super soul) Gandhi.

India is great because of its relentless pursuit of truth by Indians. Our slogan of 'Truth alone Triumphs' is a testimony to it. Therefore, take pride in being an Indian. Work hard. Work smart. Work wise to make India a prosperous country in the world. Do remember that it is an honor to be born as an Indian.

Jai Hind!

The intention of this manuscript is to enlighten readers with strengths and weaknesses so that we can overcome our weaknesses and capitalize on our strengths to make India a strong country in the world. To conclude in the words of Ratan Tata, "We have been. . . thinking small. And if we look around us, countries like China have grown so much by thinking big. I would urge that we all, in the coming years, think big, think of doing things not in small increments, not in small deltas, but seemingly impossible things. But nothing is impossible if you really set out to do so. And we act boldly. Because it is this thinking big and acting boldly that will move India up in a manner different from where it is today."

Remember: *Demonstrate patriotism.*

29

Be a Responsible Citizen

"Ask not what your country can do for you; ask what you can do for your country."

– John F. Kennedy

Dear citizen! You are the biggest resource for your nation. Do you know that? The future of your nation depends on proper utilization of your invaluable resource. Do you recognize that? You have a huge hidden potential to contribute the best for yourself and to your society. Do you realize that? When you collaborate with other citizens you can maximize your outcome and make your presence felt on your nation. Do you understand that?

If you understand these things and act accordingly, you are a responsible citizen. Remember the following points:

- Talking too much and not taking responsibility is not the quality of a good citizen.
- Neglecting your roles and responsibilities and enjoying at the cost of others is not the quality of a good citizen.
- Demanding your rights and neglecting your duties is not the responsibility of a good citizen.

Current Challenges

Presently people's expectations and aspirations are growing. They demand more and it is a tough task to meet their requirements. At times it is tough to predict their needs as they change rapidly. Therefore, all stakeholders have a tough task lying ahead.

Students demand more from teachers. Children demand more from parents. Employees demand more from employers. Followers demand more from leaders. Citizens demand more from rulers. There is need for a change in mindset from rights-orientation to duty-orientation. There must be a change in attitude. As Rome was not built in a day, it takes constant efforts and energies with an eye to deliver goods. Then, you can progress yourself and ensure the progress of your society and country as a whole.

What is in it for Me?

People often think 'what is in it for me'? They must get out of such mindset and think what difference they can make for others. Remember that what goes around comes around. If you deliver best, you get the best. It is like an echo. Hence, give your best unmindful of the outcome.

Country is nothing but a collection of people. When people work responsibly country can grow rapidly. Hence, take responsibility and move forward with energy and enthusiasm. Small countries such as Singapore and Japan made it big. Then why not India being the seventh largest country in geography; the second largest country in population; and being the largest democracy in the world make it big?

Thought Provoking Questions?

Do you pay taxes properly?

Do you take responsibility when an accident takes place on the road in front you?

Do you hand over the culprit to authorities when you find?

Do you take responsibility or pass on the buck?

Do you encourage bribe-takers?

Do you maintain cleanliness?

Are you a part of the problem or the solution?

Do you talk too much without any action?

It is time for you to take action. It is time for you to be responsible. It is time for you to clean up the mess at your level and then to clean up the system.

Some citizens often abuse the system instead of feeding it. If you don't take responsibility how can you enjoy your rights? If you don't perform your duties how can you claim your rights? Hence, cultivate the habit of contributing your best to get the best. When you take care of your duties you can enjoy your rights automatically. Remember that both duties and rights go together.

When you are the part of the problem how can you blame your country? When you don't come out with solutions how you can develop your country? Country can progress only when people act collectively with responsibility. Therefore, contribute your best to make your country proud globally. Remember the famous slogan, "People get the government they deserve." As rulers and leaders come from you, you must send good material with great attitude with a heart to contribute and serve others to make a difference.

Conclusion

Winston Churchill once remarked, "Healthy citizens are the greatest asset any country can have." Hence, be disciplined and dedicated, and respect the rights of others. Don't encroach into others' privacy. Don't enjoy at the cost of others. Above all, be a responsible citizen and contribute your best to leave a mark for yourself, your country, and mankind. My intention is to awaken and inspire you to take action for your good; for the good of your society; and your country as a whole.

Good Luck to be a Good Citizen!

> "Never doubt that a small group of thoughtful, committed citizens can change the world; indeed, it's the only thing that ever has."
>
> – *Margaret Mead*

Remember: *Be duty-oriented.*

REFERENCES

Author's Facebook Page: http://www.facebook.com/pages/Professor-MSRao/451516514937414?skip_nax_wizard=true

Author's Speaker Mix: http://speakermix.com/professor-m-s-rao

Author's Blogs:

http://professormsraoguru.blogspot.com

http://professormsrao.blogspot.com

http://profmsr.blogspot.com

> "We judge ourselves by what we feel capable of doing, while others judge us by what we have already done."
>
> – *Henry Wadsworth Longfellow*

APPENDIX-A
Students' Concerns with Clarifications

"Leadership consists of nothing but taking responsibility for everything that goes wrong and giving your subordinates credit for everything that goes well."

– Dwight D. Eisenhower

Here is a list of concerns with clarifications and questions with answers on success, personality development, life and leadership:

Q: What is the difference between nature and nurture?

A: Nature and parents gifted us many things. Talents are acquired from parents while skills are acquired by nurture. To achieve success, you must blend your talents with skills. That means you have to blend nature given gifts with skills and abilities nurturing around them.

Q: Is EQ more important than IQ?

A: Traditionally, everyone emphasized on IQ but the recent research has shown that it is the EQ that will take you to success quickly rather than the IQ. In fact, both are essential to achieve success but EQ plays a crucial role to achieve your professional and leadership success.

Q: Can you achieve success without right attitude?

A: No. Attitude is the ultimate key ingredient to achieve success. Your attitude determines your altitude of success. The difference between success and failure is attitude. Hence, emphasize on attitude to achieve success in all spheres. Remember, a person with a positive attitude with nil experience is preferred over a person with rotten attitude with great experience.

Q: How do you identify positive attitude among the candidates during interview?

A: Attitude is reflected through body postures. Hence, you must observe the body language of the candidate during interview as 55 percent of communication depends on body language while the balance 45 percent goes towards oral language and voice modulation. After asking a question observe the body cues of the candidate closely and if you find positive postures, the candidate has positive attitude and can become an asset to your organization.

Q: How do you change the attitude of individuals?

A: First of all, you must set an example for others to emulate you, and take you seriously and positively. Set goals among them so that they replace their negative thought process with positive thought process; engage themselves constructively; manage their time; and above all, stay focused to accomplish their goals. Over a period of time, people develop positive attitude.

Q: Is being a fresher a liability?

A: Not at all. Freshers have an advantage as they are on a clean slate and can be molded the way the employers want. Since they are young and receptive employers prefer them. Regarding lack of experience, remember that everyone starts from scratch. Overall, they have many advantages than experienced people. Hence, being a fresher is an asset, not a liability.

Q: Why is a lot of significance attached to only IT in India? Why not other areas?

A: You are right. Indians are traditionally strong in Mathematics and Information Technology and we have made a mark globally in these areas. That is how India has been branded globally. However, all streams and branches have opportunities. You don't have to concern about excessive importance given to IT. You pursue the areas in which you are passionate to excel greatly.

Q: What happens after death?

A: It is not known. It is better to think what you can do in your lifetime. God gifted you life, and your duty is to deliver your best to make yourself happy and the people around you. Remember that you have one life and do what best you can do in this life itself. Set your goals and work on them constantly and consistently. Above all, it is a privilege to be born as a human being. Therefore, contribute your best and make a difference in the lives of others.

Q: I don't believe in God but I want to know what happens after death.

A: Think of engaging your mind on what you can do for yourself and the society rather than thinking about death. When time comes you will leave this world. Hence, develop positive thinking and perception towards your life and provide meaning to it. Remember the sage words of Benjamin Franklin: "If you would not be forgotten as soon as you are dead, either write something worth reading or do things worth writing."

Q: How can you make your communication effective through telephone?

A: Communication consists of 7 percent oral language, 38 percent voice modulation and 55 percent body language. When you speak to the other person over telephone, you don't see the body language. Hence, you have to be more conscious on your oral language and voice modulation. Pay more attention the way you communicate, and understand the other person's voice modulation and oral language, and then create a compatibility and chemistry to ensure effective communication over telephone.

Q: How do you get the job done by a non-performer?

A: First of all, remove your perception that somebody is a non-performer. Start on a clean slate. Give the tasks and find out the areas the employee is weak. Equip him/her with skills and abilities to execute the tasks effectively. If you find that s/he is deliberately avoiding work, you need to counsel about the cons of not performing. If s/he still doesn't do the tasks deliberately then show him/her the door.

Q: How do you handle a non-performer?

A: Give him or her a long rope. Apply Chanakya's four methods of *Sama, Dhan, Bhed* and *Dandopay* to be relieved from non-performer. Remember the HR cliché: *hire slowly and fire fast.*

Q: Why do some great performers become poor performers gradually?

A: Lack of priorities and motivation may be the reasons. Employees have to set their priorities based on their passion and engage in continuous learning, unlearning and relearning to remain as great performers forever.

Q: Is it necessary to interfere when work is given?

A: The Generation Y doesn't appreciate excessive interference by others. Appropriate word for this is 'micromanagement'. Micromanagement means closely supervising the work of subordinates by superiors. Hence, give work to your subordinate and specify the time-frame and then ask for the results. Everyone has their own method of doing their work and some work fast while some work slow. It is advisable to respect people to work at their pace. When someone doesn't execute tasks due to lack of skill set you can intervene and advise.

Q: How to cope up with workplace challenges?

A: Be expert in your domain. Don't procrastinate. Be good at hard and soft skills equally. Blend your IQ (Intelligence Quotient) and EQ (Emotional Intelligence Quotient). Above all, maintain work-life balance.

Q: How to keep fire blazing among people as it often decreases as per the age and bad experiences they encounter?

A: It depends on the individuals, priorities, and their mindset. There is a term known as 'X factor' which some people possess by birth. It is a fire among them and keeps them moving forward. Such people keep the fire blazing forever and achieve greatly. Abraham Lincoln is an amazing example of keeping his fire blazing throughout his life despite facing several failures in his lifetime. Some people miss the fire when they accomplish their goals. Some people compromise and settle down when they encounter failures frequently. Hence, to keep the fire blazing, make sure that you have a broad vision with short-term, long-term and lifelong goals. Above all, make sure that you come out of your comfort zone to leave a mark behind for others to follow.

Q: How do you define leadership?

A: Leadership is the ability to lead from the front by setting an example. It is the process of setting vision, building teams, making decisions, motivating people and aligning their energies and efforts to accomplish organizational goals and objectives. Effective leadership starts with Example and ends with Ethics and imbedded throughout this process are the factors such as Energy, Enthusiasm, Endurance, Emotional Intelligence, Eloquence, Empowerment, Effectiveness, Execution, and Excellence. All are necessary to excel as a successful leader. Any shortcoming or deficiency in any one of these elements inevitably creates an imbalance in leadership effectiveness.

Q: What's the difference between management and leadership?

A: Management adopts conventional path while leadership follows unconventional path. Management is the process of doing things right while leadership is the process of doing right things.

Q: What is the difference between managers and leaders?

A: Managers are missionaries while leaders are visionaries. Managers think within the box while leaders think outside the box. Managers know how to climb the ladder while the leaders know how to place the ladder on the right side of the wall. Managers are efficient while leaders are effective.

Q: To what extent are leaders born or made?

A: It is a debatable issue globally. Most of the leaders are made rather than born because leadership is a skill that can be honed through acquisition of emotional intelligence quotient (EQ).

Q: What are the three top qualities the leaders must possess in their personality?

A: I authored a book titled, *Secrets of Your Leadership Success – The 11 Indispensable E's of a Leader* published by Shroff, in which I listed out the 11 qualities needed for leaders as follows: Example, Energy, Enthusiasm, Endurance, Emotional Intelligence, Eloquence, Empowerment, Effectiveness, Execution, Excellence and Ethics. You must set an example for others to excel as a successful leader. As a leader you are always under the scanner. Hence, your example will earn you respect and help you excel as a leader. You must have emotional intelligence to become an effective leader and above all, you must have ethics to excel as an authentic leader.

Q: If everybody is a leader, who is the follower?

A: Your question reminds me the saying, "If everybody sits in a palanquin who will lift it?" You must understand that a good follower is a good leader. If you want to be a good leader, you must be a follower first so that your followers will observe you; follow you; and accept you as a leader.

Q: How to deal with people effectively.

A: It is relevant to explain Abraham Maslow's Needs Hierarchy theory in this context as it helps understand the needs of the people to deal people effectively. Abraham Maslow was an American psychologist who created a pyramid of *Needs*

Hierarchy Theory. There are 5 levels of needs, in which people aspire next higher hierarchy of needs upon fulfillment of each level of needs. At the bottom of the pyramid, man craves for physiological needs such as food, cloth, shelter and sex. Upon fulfillment of this set of needs, man craves for next higher of needs – safety needs, as man wants to secure his life from dangers ensure physiological needs intact. After accomplishment of this need, man craves for social needs where he wants to associate with his communities, cultures, languages, and ethnicities. Then, man craves for self-esteem needs, where he wants his ego to be protected. It is rightly said that man cannot live by bread alone as he craves beyond bread and bed. At the top of the pyramid is the self-actualization needs where man likes to undertake challenging roles and responsibilities to get recognized and to stand out from others. He also likes to pursue his passions and interests. Hence, leaders must know these levels of needs and understand human psyche to succeed as effective leaders.

Q: How to balance between the seniors and juniors in the organization?

A: Currently the gap between the seniors and juniors is narrowing down. Balancing both seniors and juniors while leading is not a big challenge. You have to adopt different strokes for different folks based on their experiences. Respect the senior people and give them more challenging roles and responsibilities and make them more accountable then you can please the senior lot. At the same time, create a value system where there is no gap between the seniors and the juniors. Do remember that Generation Y appreciates equality of all as they prefer to work with partners rather than with seniors and superiors.

Q: How to handle egoistic people at the workplace?

A: Respect the egoistic people. Don't hurt them. You must learn to manage all kinds of people in the workplace. You must apply different strokes for different people. Management is all about managing the egos, emotions, and feelings of the people. Remember that people are different. You will find egoistic, adamant, arrogant, assertive and submissive people. You must understand their nature, needs, expectations, and aspirations and handle them effectively.

Q: Which skills are more important for leaders – technical or managerial skills?

A: In this context, I would like to highlight Robert Katz's three levels of management—low level, middle level and top level management. In each level of management, people need technical skills, human skills and conceptual skills in varied proportions. At low level management, people need high technical skills and low conceptual skills and fixed amount of human skills. At the middle level management, people need an equal amount of technical, conceptual and human skills. At the top level management, people need high conceptual skills, low technical skills and a fixed amount of human skills. In these three levels, the need for human skills remains constant while the need for technical and conceptual skills varies in proportion. Hence, leaders need more of conceptual skills, and it comes by experience. We can call technical skills as domain skills or hard skills, and human skills as soft skills. Succinctly, leaders need more of conceptual and soft skills and less of hard skills as they scale their corporate career ladder.

Q: What is situational leadership?

A: There are different leadership styles such as autocratic, democratic, and delegative to name a few. There is nothing like right or wrong leadership style. You have to act according to the situation, task and the people you lead. Ken Blanchard emphasized on different strokes for different folks and different strokes for same folk. People may not fall in line the way you want. Hence, you must mould your leadership style as per their needs and personalities without compromising with organizational objectives.

Q: What is the difference between transactional and transformational leadership?

A: Transactional leadership emphasizes on tasks and ends. It places more significance on production and work. In contrast, transformational leadership emphasizes on people and the means to achieve the ends. It places more significance in transforming the ordinary people into extra-ordinary people.

Q: How do the leaders make decisions - by head, heart or gut?

A: When you have full information and you need to make a decision, you can go by your head. When you have partial information, you can go by your both head and heart. When you don't have any information you can go by your gut and intuition. Above all, decision-making is situational, and it depends on the people you lead, the knowledge you have and the prevailing environment.

Q: What are the key leadership challenges in modern organizations?

A: Complexity and uncertainty are the key challenges. What worked in the past might not work in future as the times and technologies are changing rapidly. It is tough to predict what happens next. In addition, leaders must address local issues without losing sight of global issues with a broad mindset.

Q: How do you effect change smoothly?

A: People must know that change is the only thing constant in this world. The leaders must communicate clearly about the importance of change and the benefits that would bring in. They must coordinate, negotiate and facilitate to effect change smoothly and successfully to avoid resistance.

Q: Are companies really interested in developing leaders?

A: Some companies are interested while some companies are not interested. Most of the companies focus on performance not on providing training programs to their employees. It is a retrograde step. In addition, recession has become an excuse for them. The leaders at the top level must take initiative to train employees regularly to improve bottom lines and groom them as leaders. It helps retain the talent and keep cream ready in the leadership pipeline to ensure organizational excellence and effectiveness.

Q: How to become a good leader?

A: Keep working hard. Do your job without expecting any returns. Spread the fame during success and take the blame during failures. Make a difference in the lives of others. Handhold and groom others as leaders. I am sure you will excel as a good leader.

Q: What leadership attributes are required in this globalized world?

A: Technology has made the world into a small village. It brought comforts as well as confusion. Hence, leaders must adopt flexibility and adaptability to manage complexity and uncertainty. They must respect all cultures and communities and catch up with the latest technology. Above all, they have to learn, unlearn and relearn to stand out.

Q: In which way the technology will influence the leaders?

A: Presently there is a tremendous influence of technology as we have virtual teams and virtual leaders. The leaders must get updated with the latest technology. They must change with the changing times and technologies. Thanks to technology that I reach out to people through webinars and internet! There is growing complexity and uncertainty currently. The globe has become a small village. Therefore, leaders must unlearn, learn and relearn to get updated with technology to grow as global leaders.

Q: Do leaders groom others as leaders?

A: Yes. Real leaders groom others as leaders. They deliver their best. They make a difference in the lives of others. When you look at *Level 5 Leaders* coined by Jim Collins, they are highly passionate and don't mind who takes credit for their contribution. They build leaders around them so that they can groom leaders and undertake higher roles and responsibilities. They want to keep the leadership pipeline unclogged. As parents groom their children, the authentic leaders groom others as leaders.

Q: How do you learn from others' failures?

A: The famous poet, Archibald MacLeish once said, "There is only one thing more painful than learning from experience, and that is not learning from experience." When you look at leaders like Ronald Reagan and Abraham Lincoln they encountered several failures in their lives but they made it big at the end because they did not take failures personally. They learned lessons from their experience and achieved greatly at the end. They made wrong decisions, learned lessons, and improved their subsequent decision making and achieved success ultimately. If you learn from their experiences your success rate as a leader will enhance.

Q: How do we develop the next generation of leaders?

A: You cannot become a crackshot unless you lose some ammunition. Empower your employees. Encourage them to take risk and explore. Do your duty and don't expect rewards. Believe in contribution, not accumulation. Cultivate the attitude of gratitude.

Q: What is sandwich feedback?

A: Sandwich feedback is a polished way of giving feedback to others. It starts by praising strengths, then suggesting improvements, and concluding with praise. Precisely, it is putting the tough news between the two tender positive pieces of feedback. In this feedback, you must attack the behavior of the individuals, not the individuals to achieve the desired outcomes. It doesn't hurt the receivers as the criticism is well sandwiched. The receivers take what is really needed and develop the attitude of gratitude towards the feedback giver.

Q: What is the top quality needed for a trainer?

A: A trainer must be passionate, committed, and dedicated. If you have passion to bring out the behavioral changes among the participants, you are a successful trainer. Don't bother about their feedback. Deliver your best and ensure effective takeaways. There are trainers who use excessive humor to keep participants happy during the program and walk away with good feedback. They don't ensure takeaways among participants. You must ensure effective takeaways among them by accomplishing the training objectives. Remember that training is not a popularity contest. If you are not passionate, don't enter into this profession.

Q: How to take responsibilities when others don't allow us to shoulder them?

A: Yes. It is the challenge some of the leaders encounter. Theoretically, we say many things but practically things happen in its own way. You cannot become a crackshot unless you lose some ammunition. You must undergo this painful process to let the leader within you emerge. The more you encounter such challenges the more you build your emotional quotient (EQ) and greater the chance to excel as a good leader.

Q: How can you work under people who criticize? How to excel as a leader among them?

A: Leadership is not a cakewalk. It is replete with bouquets and brickbats. You must be in a position to take both equally. You will find people praising and criticizing you everywhere. When you demonstrate your integrity and adopt ethics, people around you realize your true intentions over a period of time, and they respect you and accept you as a leader. However, it is easier said than done. When you overcome critics the real leadership potential comes to the surface. This is the silver lining on the dark cloud of leadership.

Q: What is the best hierarchy for leadership?

A: There is nothing like the best hierarchy. It all depends on the vision and mission of the company. It also depends on the type of products or services and the presence the company has globally. Nowadays, employees and especially, Gen Y appreciate lean and flat structure with limited hierarchy.

Q: How can leaders build their energy and enthusiasm?

A: It is individual specific. In general, you can build your energy and enthusiasm when you enter into your passionate areas as you don't feel working hard. You can also build by doing mediation, through solitude, hitting gym, and pursuing games and sports. They will renew your energy and enthusiasm thus enhancing your performance. Remember that enthusiasm is the real asset that you can pass on to your children as it helps them face challenges head-on and keeps them moving them forward successfully.

Q: You authored a book, *21 Success Sutras for Leaders* published by Pearson. Do these sutras apply in every profession?

A: Here are the 21 sutras for your leadership success which have been distilled from my extensive reading, intensive compilation and from my 32 years of experience and expertise in various areas:

1. Leadership is a Responsibility, not a Badge of Honor.
2. Character Counts, not Charisma.
3. Be a Coach, not a Critic.
4. Build Bridges, not Barriers.
5. Fight for Pretty Things, not Petty Things.
6. Strive for Excellence, not Perfection.
7. Failure is only a Comma, not a Full Stop.
8. Never Say 'No' too Soon and 'Yes' too Late.
9. Praise Publicly and Punish Privately.
10. Spread the Fame in Success and Take the Blame in Failure.
11. Listen to all and Take Your Call.
12. Walk Your Talk.
13. Deal People Differently.
14. Leaders Command Respect.
15. Don't Blame Circumstances.

16. Don't Compete, Collaborate.
17. Don't React, Act.
18. Think Global, Act Local.
19. Invest in People.
20. Everybody is a Leader.
21. Soft Leadership is the Heart of Leadership.

These 21 success sutras can be applied everywhere irrespective of the profession - whether you are a business leader, political leader, religious leader or a military leader. However, you must customize them as per the sector, industry, the area of activity you are into and the people you lead. When you understand these concepts well you will be able to apply as per the profession, situation, and the people around you, you will achieve your leadership effectiveness and success.

Q: What kind of leaders the present American leaders are?

A: Leadership is individual specific, not country specific. However, when you look at the present President of America, Barack Obama, he is a charismatic leader who rose from humble origins. He has the gift of the gab. Charisma plays a crucial role for American leaders. Most of the American leaders believe in democratic leadership and they prefer to work in teams. It again differs from leader to leader. Americans expect their leaders to be enterprising and charming who can influence and inspire them. They appreciate their leaders to be adventurous and risk takers.

Q: Why are we Indians not producing leaders globally?

A: Indian culture and mindset is different. We create more managers rather than leaders. However, the Gen Y is smarter lot and is doing great. They have an immense fire and exposed to technology and are very fast in thinking. I am sure we will produce more leaders globally in the years to come. I am bullish and optimistic about Gen Y who can put India on the global map by leading from the front. Presently, we have so many global leadership gurus in the Thinkers 50. Once C.K. Prahlad was ranked # 1 thinker in this list, and presently we have Vijay

Govindarajan who has been ranked as the # 3 management thinker in the world. When you look at the latest list of Thinkers 50 – 2011, it is obvious that there are a growing number of Indian gurus globally. It is a silver lining in the dark cloud for India.

Q: Why politicians are considered leaders in India?

A: Indian politicians are better at emotional intelligence quotient (EQ) because they cultivate it through their experience although some of them may have low intelligence quotient (IQ). You will also find some of them without formal education. Similarly, there are non-MBAs who are CEOs. There are college dropouts who are CEOs because they have entrepreneurial zeal and succeeded as leaders due to high EQ. At the same time, there are a number of MBAs who are employees. Hence, you must understand that although some people may not have good education they can still grow as leaders. So is the case with Indian politicians. Remember that leadership is not a popularity contest. Popularity is a passing cloud. Real leaders learn lessons from their mistakes and from others' mistakes and improve their decision-making. They want to serve others without any expectations. They develop more leaders around them and make a difference in the lives of others.

Q: What is your definition of a successful leader? Post-recession, will leadership look at running their companies differently?

A: Successful leader is the one who copes up with complexity and uncertainty in the current world. He must be competent in cross-cultural issues. He must have a global mindset with a local touch. He must collaborate rather than compete, and must look at similarities rather than differences among the people. He must handhold his people and be prepared to take the blame in case of failures, and spread the fame in case of successes.

Recession is a boon in disguise. Historically several companies were born during great depression and recession. Leaders must learn to convert the so-called threat of recession into an opportunity. In addition, leaders must learn lessons from their mistakes and must think out-of-the-box to come out with innovative ideas and solutions. The companies must shed their flab and get trim and slim. It is time for companies to take stock of the situation and grab the opportunities. Leaders must design new tools and techniques to come out of recession. Of course, it is easier said than done.

Q: What are the principle concerns that need to be looked at when designing a leadership development programme to solidify organizational success?

A: It is essential to conduct training needs analysis by companies to know what employees lack currently within the organization. Having known the reasons for lack of leadership they must hire passionate researchers and trainers who can find out what is really required in the current context. They must also forecast the future requirements for leaders. Companies must spot their employees with potential to grow as leaders who demonstrate leadership spark and X factor. They must look at the background of the employees and groom them as leaders. Since the baby boomers are resigning there is a looming leadership crisis arising globally as Gen X is not ready to take up leadership roles and responsibilities. Hence, companies must design their own leadership development programs (LDPs) to train and groom leaders ready in the leadership pipeline to avert organizational eventuality.

Q: What pressures and challenges does rapid growth pose for leadership programmes?

A: Globally companies are busy with their own challenges to beat competition due to the rising expectations and aspirations of their clients and customers. They are already beset with such challenges and pressures, and are not focusing on leadership development programs (LDP). At the same time the employees prefer to work in companies that promote their career growth. Research reveals that most of the employees prefer career growth to compensation package because employees are of the opinion that if there is quick career advancement the compensation package will follow automatically. Therefore, it is a huge task for companies to balance between the clients' expectations for better products and services, and the employees' aspirations for career advancement through learning and development programs.

Q: How can a company's talent management strategy be aligned to senior leadership goals for maximum impact?

A: Talent management has a crucial role to play to retain the best talent and to train them for future organizational requirements. Talent management must design a long term vision and strategy based on the vision and mission of the company, and must work with senior leadership to achieve maximum outcomes. The leaders must encourage Talent Conversations with their employees to build bridges and to know their pulse. The Talent Conversations is also known as touch time in the corporate world. It is essential to build a competency-based model by taking inventory of existing talents and skills of their employees and link them as per the organizational goals and objectives. There must be effective coordination between talent management and senior leadership within the organization to align both short-term and long-term objectives to achieve maximum impact.

Q: In your view, is there a lack of urgency in organizations to improve performance based on the idea that current level of leadership skill is adequate?

A: Yes. The companies must change their current complacency mindset. In fact, they are busy fighting with day-to-day challenges, and don't find time to develop leaders. They realize when they are faced with leadership-talent deficit arising due to the exit of precious leadership talent. Hence, companies must view it seriously, and spend adequate time for developing leaders apart from fighting regular corporate challenges. They must understand the ground realities and speed up LDP not only to make their employees grow professionally but also to keep their leadership pipeline flowing continuously.

Q: How does a leader ensure that he has an engaged employee base and how does he put metrics in place to track effectiveness?

A: Leaders must connect with their employees constantly and get to know developments constantly. It helps them know the engaged employees and design their strategies to track effectiveness. In fact, connection is the key to leadership effectiveness and success.

Q: Which firms in India do you regard as leaders in the talent development field? What are a few things that distinguish them?

A: There are several Indian companies who are the leaders in the talent development field. I would like to highlight about L&T in this regard. L&T came out with a 5-step leadership development process for incubating the company's top leadership talent. It invested heavily in leadership development of its precious manpower. It encourages the talented employees to grow as leaders and keeps them in the leadership pipeline. At each step, it engages prestigious companies and global business schools including Harvard Business School to develop its leadership talent. The process helps the company develop its leadership talent not only to meet its organizational standards but also live up to global standards.

It roped in McKinsey consultancy to develop its leaders. The LDP will identify 40-odd senior managers eventually who will then be mentored continuously by board members. It is grooming the next set of leaders to fill the present leadership vacuum. As per the plan, McKinsey will analyze performance of senior managers and suggest a career path for them. Every year a handful of them would be sent to Harvard Business School and London Business School to hone their management skills.

Q: Does global reach make it more challenging for leaders, and how has globalization affected leadership development efforts in Indian corporations?

A: The world has become a global village due to rapid changes in technologies, and it is a tough task for leaders. At the same time it is a great opportunity for leaders as they are connected with the world quickly. We get to know everything at the click of a mouse. Leaders must learn to accept change, and facilitate change keeping the current complexity, uncertainty and globalization in view. Above all, they must convert challenges into opportunities.

Q: Diversity and gender parity in hiring is an issue in most firms today. What should firms be doing to bridge the relative absence of women in the ranks?

A: These are the thorny organizational issues globally. Very few women are leading from the front leaving exceptions like Indra Nooyi, the Chairman & CEO of PepsiCo. There is glass ceiling still existing in the corporate world currently. Women should break it to come on par with male leaders and it takes some time. Presently there are great initiatives globally in these two areas of diversity and gender. There is need to encourage diversity as it helps in innovation as diversified employees bring new ideas and solutions that help innovate successfully and stay ahead of competition.

Q: You have talent that goes to work elsewhere or has retired. Is it a good idea for the leader to maintain relationships with them?

A: Nothing is permanent in the world, neither the positions nor the companies. People keep changing companies due to various reasons. It is good to maintain relations with others because the world is very small. Remember, what goes around comes around. Hence, leaders must keep in touch with the talent.

Q: What are the initiatives in leadership development programs (LDPs) globally?

A: There are global companies that took great initiative in grooming leaders through LDP such as General Electric, Procter & Gamble, American Express, Colgate, PepsiCo, and Sherwin-Williams, Textron Southwest Airlines, 3M, and Zappos to name a few. P&G runs leadership development program titled *Inspirational Leadership* and *American Express* runs a program called 'Leadership Inspiring Employee Engagement'. Likewise, few prestigious international companies have coined different names to their leadership development programs and rolled out keeping their vision and mission in view. They developed their employees regularly through LDPs; improved their bottom lines; and excelled as employee-friendly companies. They have kept leadership pipeline unclogged to ensure smooth supply of leaders to enhance organizational excellence and effectiveness. For instance, Jack Welch, the former CEO and chairman of General Electric, is an amazing example of a leader who built leaders around himself. He was a brilliant coach and mentor to the leaders who reported to him and contributed greatly to their development and the success of their business units and functions. He made his success plan clear by grooming Jeff Immelt for the top slot. Similarly, Steve Jobs prepared Timothy Cook to the top slot for Apple when he was nearing to death due to cancer.

Q: What are the steps and strategies to be adopted to ensure successful rolling out of leadership development programs (LDPs) globally?

A: To roll out the LDP, there is no quick fix formula as such but companies can adopt a series of strategies and steps to customize and develop their employees. Here is the five-step process to proceed:

1. Recruit the leadership researchers and trainers who are passionate in learning and development and who can make a difference.
2. Ask them to do intensive research about the current and future needs of companies and design course content accordingly. They must not blindly follow training techniques that worked in the past, and also that of other companies because what worked in the past may now work now, and what worked for others may not work for them as the needs, times and technologies are changing rapidly.

3. Involve the senior leaders within the company to undertake training programs so that they can share their experiences with their employees and also connect with them at the ground level. For instance, Jack Welch conducted teaching assignments in GE. Besides, to teach is to learn twice as the leaders prepare thoroughly to facilitate the training program and get to know the challenges within the companies from the ground level. Above all, they can inspire their employees with their active participation.
4. Take feedback after each LDP about its relevance to ensure effective takeaways. For instance, post course improvement measurement is an imperative to plug the existing gaps both in the course content and delivery to deliver better in the next training session. As Ken Blanchard rightly remarked, feedback is the breakfast of champions, and timely feedback ensures updated course content plan with latest delivery in training methodologies.
5. Follow-up thoroughly to make training process and procedures better. If there are any deficiencies, address them immediately and move on. The process has to be repeated after each LDP. Remember that leaders are developed daily, not in a day. Leadership development is a long drawn process keeping both short-term and long-term goals in view. Hence, companies must realize that developing leaders is a way of life to address leadership-deficit and to leave a legacy behind. Great leaders appreciate leaving a good legacy rather than inheriting from others.

Q: What is your vision?

A: I want to share my knowledge with the world. Hence, I created three blogs http://professormsraoguru.blogspot.com http://professormsrao.blogspot.com, and http://profmsr.blogspot.com and a Facebook page http://www.facebook.com/pages/Professor-MSRao/451516514937414?skip_nax_wizard=true to share my knowledge online and also through teaching and training programs. My long-term vision is to train 1,000,000 people and develop them as leaders. I want to make a difference in the lives of others and to the society as a whole. I want to promote global peace and prosperity. I coined a new leadership perspective - "Soft Leadership" and want to apply it in all areas to make people important and special so that they can wholeheartedly contribute for the benefit of mankind.

Q: What is your message to the world?

A: Love your mother, but don't hate another person's mother. Love your community but don't hate another person's community. Look at similarities, not differences. Above all, make a difference in the lives of others.

REFERENCES

Author's Facebook Page: http://www.facebook.com/pages/Professor-MSRao/451516514937414?skip_nax_wizard=true

Author's Speaker Mix: http://speakermix.com/professor-m-s-rao

Author's Blogs:

http://professormsraoguru.blogspot.com

http://professormsrao.blogspot.com

http://profmsr.blogspot.com

References

Introducing NLP Sue Knight, Universities Press

Decision Making - Harvard Business Review Series

Online References

Author's Facebook Page: http://www.facebook.com/pages/Professor-MSRao/451516514937414?skip_nax_wizard=true

Author's Speaker Mix: http://speakermix.com/professor-m-s-rao

Author's Blog: http://profmsr.blogspot.com

Author's Blog: http://professormsrao.blogspot.com

Author's Blog: http://professormsraoguru.blogspot.com

http://www.youngentrepreneur.com/blog/100-top-entrepreneurs-who-succeeded-without-a-college-degree/

Key Points

1. Identify the spark within you to achieve all-round success.
2. Cultivate the mindset of an achiever by building a positive, right and strong attitude.
3. Emphasize on extracurricular activities in the educational institution to excel as a leader
4. Acquire the career acumen and follow the road less traveled.
5. Build knowledge, skills and abilities needed for industry to enhance your employment opportunities.
6. Work hard, smart and wise to fast-track your career.
7. Set SMART goals and hit bull's eye to leave a mark behind for others to follow.
8. Change your mindset to face challenges squarely and successfully.
9. Identify the thin line and cross it to achieve the expected outcomes.
10. Be good with books and hands to achieve success greatly.
11. Differentiate between job seeker and job provider and prefer to become an entrepreneur.
12. Get inspired by entrepreneurs who excelled without proper education and explore entrepreneurial opportunities.

13. Emphasize quality, not quantity to achieve excellence.
14. Understand the importance of soft skills at each level of management to become CEO quickly.
15. Build compatibility and chemistry by molding yourself with the help of Neuro-Linguistic Programming (NLP).
16. Clarify your queries by asking right and intelligent questions.
17. Address listening challenges effectively to excel as a leader.
18. Present positive body language to connect with others quickly and win their confidence.
19. Apply assertive tools and techniques to ensure better productivity and performance in the workplace.
20. Adopt sandwich technique to decline requests firmly but politely.
21. Understand the personality type of your boss and be in his or her books to ensure your professional survival and success.
22. Make your decision wisely by blending your head, heart and gut.
23. Don't blame circumstances and work with what you have.
24. Balance your personal, professional and social life proportionately to achieve success and lead your life successfully.
25. Broaden your circle of friends to build your network.
26. Build your leadership brand, enhance your market value and make a difference in the lives of others.
27. Look at the similarities, not differences to promote fraternity and brotherhood globally.
28. Demonstrate patriotism and serve your country.
29. Be duty-oriented rather than rights-oriented to make your country prosperous.

Epilogue

"Books are the quietest and most constant of friends; they are the most accessible and wisest of counselors, and the most patient of teachers."

–Charles William Eliot

I have authored this book to offer success sutras for students to stay inspired and to achieve professional success. If this book helps you achieve your expectations, it will have done its job. If you put this book down feeling that you are better equipped to become a successful professional and leader, I feel that my work as an author has been accomplished.

I would appreciate your valuable feedback to make improvements to this book. You may post your feedback at http://speakermix.com/professor-m-s-rao Facebook Page: http://www.facebook.com/pages/Professor-MSRao/451516514937414?skip_nax_wizard=true or send me an e-mail: profmsr13@gmail.com. If you want information on the seminars and workshops on leadership that I conduct or my availability as a speaker for your group or conference, please contact me. You may also visit my Blogs http://profmsr.blogspot.com, http://professormsrao.blogspot.com, and http://professormsraoguru.blogspot.com which are read globally. These blogs pertain to Learning, Leadership, Coaching, and Soft Skills. Please post your comments directly on the blogs themselves, as it helps others appreciate your ideas. If you find the blogs interesting, please share the links with your friends, as knowledge grows when shared.

You may share your thoughts about *Success Sutras for Students: Stay Inspired!* on Facebook, Twitter, LinkedIn, and the websites you visit. You can also blog about it or write a book review.

I pray for your success.

Professor M.S.Rao

Founder, MSR Leadership Consultants India

About The Author

Professor M.S.Rao,
International Leadership Guru
Blogs: http://profmsr.blogspot.com
http://professormsrao.blogspot.com
http://professormsraoguru.blogspot.com

Professor M.S.Rao is an international leadership guru who rose from humble origins. He is recognized as one of the world's leading leadership educators, authors, speakers, coaches, consultants and practitioners. He has 32 years of experience in leadership development, and conducts leadership development training programs for various corporates and educational institutions. He is an Executive Coach and Motivational Speaker, and delivers guest lectures upon request. He coined a new leadership tool – *Soft Leadership Grid;* leadership teaching tool – *11E Leadership Grid;* and innovative teaching tool – *Meka's Method*. His areas of interest include Leadership, Coaching, and Learning and Development.

He is the Founder of MSR Leadership Consultants, India and the author of 21 books including the award-winning book *21 Success Sutras for Leaders*. He has published more than 250 papers and articles in international publications including *Leader to Leader, Leadership Excellence, T+D Magazine (ASTD), Personal Excellence, Chief Learning Officer Magazine, Emerald,* and *Sage*. He serves as an Advisor and Board Member for several prestigious international organizations including American Institute of Business Psychology (AIOBP), USA, and Global Leadership Awards, Malaysia. He has been listed as one of the leading achievers around the world in *Marquis Who's Who in the World* in 2013. He successfully led a webinar as a thought leader on Soft Leadership: A New Leadership Perspective organized by International Leadership Association, America.

He serves on the editorial boards of various prestigious international journals including *Development and Learning in Organizations* and *Industrial and Commercial Training*, of Emerald Journals—U.K., *International Journal of Business Administration*—Canada, and *Journal of Business Studies Quarterly*—USA. He is ranked as No.1 among the speakers in India as per reviews on Speakerpedia URL: http://speakerpedia.com/speakers/professor-msrao. He can be reached at: profmsr13@gmail.com and additionally maintains three popular blogs titled 'Where Knowledge is Wealth'—URL http://profmsr.blogspot.com, 'Professor M.S.Rao Born for the Students'—URL http://professormsrao.blogspot.com and 'Knowledge Grows When Shared'—URL http://professormsraoguru.blogspot.com